Michael **Aspel**
IN GOOD COMPANY

Michael
Aspel
IN GOOD COMPANY

Robson Books

With many thanks to all my special guests, to everybody on the *Aspel* production teams and grateful thanks to Sue Thomas and Lorna Dickinson, without whose valuable help the book could never have been written

First published in Great Britain in 1989 by Robson Books Ltd, Bolsover House, 5–6 Clipstone Street, London W1P 7EB

Copyright © 1989 London Weekend Television

British Library Cataloguing in Publication Data
Aspel, Michael
  In good company.
  1. Great Britain. Entertainments. Aspel, Michael –
Biographies
  I. Title
  791'.092'4

  ISBN 0 86051 597 4

Typeset by Bookworm Typesetting, Manchester
Printed in Great Britain by Biddles Ltd., Guildford and King's Lynn

CONTENTS

ANOTHER DAY – ANOTHER TALK SHOW HOST

It was a journalist from one of the Sunday papers who raised the question. 'Don't you think there are too many talk shows around?' she asked. 'There certainly are,' I said. 'The others should stop at once.' Unfortunately nobody's yet taken the hint.

The idea for me to enter the arena came long before the first *Aspel and Company* ever hit the screen. I'd always wanted, in a slightly masochistic way, to do a talk show. I'd been a news reader and a disc jockey; I'd been a reporter and a radio actor; and I'd gone round sticking microphones up the noses of people at Royal film premières and Miss World contests until I felt I couldn't do it any longer. I'd interviewed many people on the radio – and enjoyed it, too – but a television talk show was something I hadn't done. Even the title came ready-made, from an afternoon show that I'd done many years earlier with the BBC. It seemed to fit the bill – it got my name in, and it said what the show was about. So there was London Weekend Television, in the summer of 1983, with the idea, the title and a host who was willing and felt reasonably able.

It took the best part of a year before the idea became an actual programme. First, we considered the competition. Michael Parkinson wasn't doing a lot at the time, Terry Wogan had a Saturday night show, dear old Russell Harty was around then, but there was certainly room for one more.

Now, when I'm brave enough to think about it, it occurs to me that it's a strange thing that people should want to watch people simply talking to one another. Very odd – but rather like eavesdropping, I suppose, and we all like a bit of that. Also, while

9

there are probably more 'stars' around than ever, the number of Hollywood Greats has lessened. Cinema is still huge, but television reaches more people, and home-grown stars like David Jason can be every bit as popular as actors from the big screen. Also, those self-same Hollywood Greats are a different breed these days. They've discovered the phrase, 'A Private Person'. Unfortunately, that often means that any interesting chat goes right out the window. It means that whenever somebody's absolutely terrified, or thinks he's rather too important to talk about the mundane details of everyday life, then he takes refuge in the phrase, 'I'm a very private person.' And sometimes in retrospect I wish they'd not gone public.

Still, I like talking to people and I wanted to have a stab at doing it on television. On radio, it was heartening to know that the guests who came on the show did so because they felt they'd get a good and fair hearing. I did my homework, I was keen to meet them and I enjoyed their company.

So it came as a great shock to me to discover, with the first series of *Aspel and Company*, that I had never been so scared in my life. Here I was, 50 years old, I'd been around a while, I was used to interviewing celebrities, and to being on television. It shouldn't have frightened me, but it did.

You always imagine the first show will be the worst, but we had the best of possible starts. Paul McCartney plus Tracey Ullman with Richard Clayderman on keyboard – not a bad line-up by anyone's standards. Paul hadn't done a talk show before so that was a real first, and at the end of the programme, he, Tracey and I sang 'That'll Be The Day' together. What a start – except that afterwards, Paul said, 'You were nervous, weren't you?' And he was perfectly right. But I realized at that moment, with some dismay, that it must have shown.

I've often wondered exactly what I got so scared about, although there's no denying that the talk show is a very exposed area. You're under attack from the word go and if you're slightly nervous – and I was more than slightly nervous – then you find that it doesn't work. And that's when the critics start honing their daggers. It does tend to sap your confidence and your vitality, particularly when you agree with the critics. You have to watch yourself afterwards, no matter how painful it is, because a series like *Aspel and Company* is hopefully an ongoing thing, and you've got to get it right.

I was also labouring under the stigma of a programme called *The*

Monday Show many years ago, which was a fiasco. It was a half-regional, half-national, early evening show – it began locally and had the rest of the country joining in half-way through. The producer thought it would be a good idea not to have famous people as guests, but to have interesting ordinary people, like poetry-writing dustmen. Well, it didn't work, and it took a long time for me to get over it, but I thought that time, and my experience of interviewing on the radio, plus a little show called *Ask Aspel* which I had done for some years for BBC Children's TV, had given me back my confidence.

On radio, however, you can go to a record or a commercial break if things get sticky. And then during those breaks, you can plan the rest of the interview, or just take a deep breath. But neither of those safety nets are available under the obelisk eye of the camera. I knew I had a lot to beat, but I also knew that I could get people to talk, and that was what made the first show such a deep disappointment. I'd had years of people leaving the studio saying 'I've enjoyed our talk,' and I knew that I'd done a good job. So when I suddenly found myself sitting there, sweating and asking questions that I would never normally have dreamed of asking, then I thought to myself: 'My boy, you've lost it.'

Much later, when the show and I were into our stride, Wayne Sleep was a guest and he talked about the pain of being a dancer. He said, 'At least Sebastian Coe can look absolutely exhausted as he runs to the tape. I always think of dancing as being like running the hundred yards with a smile on your face.'

And I think that just about sums up how I felt during those first shows.

LADIES AND GENTLEMEN, PLEASE WELCOME...

Some months before each series, there is a frantic period of preparation. We draw up the perfect guest list, and then go about extending the invitations – we haven't yet resorted to blackmail but it can only be a matter of time. For every guest who actually appears on the show, there have been dozens of telephone calls. We begin by finding out exactly what's going on – what films and plays are due to open, books to be published, records to be released, and we keep in touch with agents and promotion companies and keep tabs on where the big celebrities are in the world.

Choosing the names is the easiest part. We can all think of the favourites, and if I could get the Pope, Frank Sinatra and the Queen I'd book them tomorrow. We begin by drawing up a huge 'A' list of all the stars that everybody recognizes, and that would always include the Royal family and such people as Paul Newman, Robert Redford, Jackie Onassis, and so on. I wouldn't object to a few ex-Presidents – Dickie and Ronnie and the lads would have some fascinating tales. The Duke and Duchess of Windsor would have been marvellous and I suspect they might have done it, too. Agreeing on names is harder. Occasionally someone on the team will say, 'Oh, we must have so-and-so,' and someone else will shout back, 'You must be joking, I can't stand him!' In the end, we seek a second opinion – either we go out and accost a taxi driver, or we'll ring our families, who are so accustomed to being used as sounding boards that they are beginning to insist on a screen credit.

When we've decided on the names, we then have to find the best person to approach for each potential guest, and that can be like a detective job. In America these days stars don't just have an agent, they have publicity assistants and managers and accountants, who are becoming increasingly important. Nobody ever got rich by just going on talk shows – well, not on mine, anyway – and when you're talking about actors who are paid millions of pounds for one film, then I suspect their accountants advise them against it. Their publicity people, on the other hand, will see the advantages. In special circumstances we'll cover some expenses and we pay them a token fee, which a lot of guests donate to charity.

We've now started to make forays into America when we're looking for guests. A member of our research team will show a tape of one of the programmes and hopefully that will persuade whoever it may be that it might not be such a bad thing to appear on it. Certainly Americans see it as being very different from their home-grown shows and for some reason they all seem to think that I ask rather cheeky questions, which I'll take as a compliment. The point is that if you just ring America, you might as well be from outer Albania for all they care. They have their own talk shows, and British TV is just one more headache. They tend to say, 'Can't we do one satellite interview that covers the whole of Europe?' That's where I envy people like Johnny Carson, the most famous chat show host in America – and therefore the world. Most of the guests on his show live next door – they just pop in on the way home from work. They go on again and again and so Carson never has to sit at their feet. He doesn't have to break any ice because they're all pals. It's just chat – how's the family, here's the latest joke, how's it going – and that somehow makes for great entertainment.

Once a celebrity has agreed to be a guest, the researcher assigned to him or her will go along for an exploratory conversation. This hopefully will provide a wealth of reminiscence and anecdote, and might take place anywhere from Putney to Paris. The furthest anyone has had to travel was to Los Angeles and back, all in forty-eight hours, to persuade the reclusive Harrison Ford to appear on the show. Once the researcher arrived though, Harrison was as friendly as you like, showed her around the house that he built himself, even showed her the pictures he'd painted, and best of all, agreed to be a guest on *Aspel and Company*. A rather unhappier experience awaited the researcher who flew to Paris to interview Jodie Foster – she caught food poisoning on the plane and was ill throughout their meeting. Since then Jodie tends to sit at a separate table for interviews.

After asking them all about their latest film, their hobbies, their lovers, wives, husbands, children, and anything else of interest, our researchers will come back with their tape-recorded notes, pick out the best bits of their interview and write up a biography. It usually ends up like a cross between *The Sun*'s 'Things You Never Knew' column and *The Times Literary Review*. This can be anything from five pages on someone like Dame Edna Everage – because she's a fictional person (or didn't you know?) to thirty or forty pages for the Elizabeth Taylors of the world. And that's not all the researchers will be doing. They'll find out, for example, that Julio Iglesias prefers to be filmed only from the right – which could be useful for the cameramen. Or if we're thinking of inviting an up-and-coming actor on the show, the researchers will find tapes of them being interviewed, usually from America, in order for us to watch them in action. Someone who's brilliant on the cinema screen isn't necessarily a good talk show guest. Indeed, one of the researchers' most important tasks is to ascertain for my benefit what kind of conversation we'll be likely to have – whether the guest talks nineteen to the dozen, in which case I'll need to prepare lots of questions, or if they take ten minutes to say 'Good evening' - in which case I'll start praying.

It's very different on radio, which is where I've had most of my interviewing experience. For a radio interview, I'd do my own homework, and I've always believed in doing it thoroughly. Sometimes it seemed I knew more about my guests than they did themselves. At the beginning of *Aspel and Company* I felt a bit daunted by this team of brilliant people who were, in some ways, doing my legwork for me, and the odd hiccup still arises from having lots of people on the case. Like the time when we were having a well-established film star on the show, and the researcher suggested that I should say as an opening gambit, 'You're still a very attractive man, aren't you?' 'I can't say that,' I said. And she said, 'But he *is* a very attractive man,' and I said, 'Yes, but you're a 22 year-old girl and I'm – well, I'm not.'

I have come to appreciate over the years, however, that the extra material they provide makes a great safety net. I still add my own research, and usually something will come up during the course of the interview that means you can leave the game plan anyway. The material researchers provide makes a great safety net. I still add my own research, and usually something will come up during the course of the interview that means you can leave the game plan anyway. The worst thing an interviewer can do is stick rigidly to the questions, without really listening to the answers. Clive James summed it up when he said, 'It's one thing to ask the question but you've got to listen to the answer so that your next question follows on. Otherwise you'll ask a question like, "What did you do at school?" and he'll say, "Well, I was planning the Great Train Robbery and I murdered my mother ..." And then you'll say, "And then I suppose you went to university?" '

There are always moments however, when you're extremely grateful for those planned guidelines. The mind can go horribly blank, especially when you're thinking, 'Did I hear that right? Suppose I ask such and such, and why is the floor manager waving his arms about?' You may not think the end result worth it, but there are an awful lot of balls to be kept in the air and some fairly nasty consequences if any should accidentally hit the ground.

The thing about talk shows is that you just never know how they'll turn out. It all depends on the mood of the guest, the combination of people we have on, and a million other unforeseeable factors. A 'good' guest, one who'll really deliver the goods, has to play the game. It means knowing what the show requires and not what their ego needs. When you've got a Mel Smith on or a Michael Caine or a George Melly, then you know it's going to be all right. I remember Lauren Bacall talking on the show about her idea of a real man. She said a real man is someone who knows what he's about, who knows himself and can be relaxed about himself, and I think the same could be said about the ideal guest.

Some guests, like Mel Brooks, are going to give a performance – you know that before they come on, but you also know that there will be a semblance of conversation. I'm very fond of Mel, although he's given me some hard times. The first time I met him was on radio. 'You've got a much bigger nose than I expected, Michael,' he said. '*Isn't* that a lovely dress you're wearing – and the shoes with goldfish in the heels – divine.' When he came on *Aspel and Company*, he got me again. Now we never set up questions on the show – we'll discuss areas that we might go into, but we never say, 'You say this to me, and then I'll say that to you', it just doesn't work like that. Except on one occasion. Mel said to me, 'When we do it,

Bill Martin, our truly professional warm-up man.

A new singing star? That'll be the day! Paul McCartney
and Tracy Ullman.

The drinks are on Paul, at the end of the very first show.

A rare privilege: sharing a joke with the PM.

Mrs Thatcher rubs shoulders with Barry Manilow.

Sigourney Weaver, The Joan Collins' Fan Club and a bemused
Robert Kilroy-Silk.

ask me about my father. Say, "You lost him at an early age, didn't you?" and I'll say, "Lost him? Michael, if I'd lost him I'd have gone out to look for him – he died." ' It wasn't that funny, but I agreed. Some months later I got a cheque for six hundred dollars – apparently a programme in America had done a feature on what can happen when you ask a stupid question and that was my fee for being included. On reflection, it was probably the easiest six hundred dollars I'll ever make.

Michael Caine and I always have a good rapport. We're exactly the same age, and have similar backgrounds, so we're on common ground from the start. Talking to him is always like meeting him for the first time – he never comes out with the same old stuff and you can look forward to an interesting conversation. There are quite a few Americans who go on talk shows and simply give a performance. They forget that the magic of television means that we've probably heard it all before, so we really do make an effort to go for fresh material. When we had Arthur Marshall, Dirk Bogarde and Joanna Lumley on the show together it was different. Instead of the stock stories about Bogarde's early films, we went for a bit of drama as he lives in France and Arthur Marshall hated the French. Dirk is an excellent guest. I remember once when he was talking about acting on the continent, he said, 'They like me because I act like a German.' I said, 'You mean, you push to the front of queues. . . .' He was man enough to smile, and it made Arthur Marshall laugh, which was always a wonderful sight.

Alan Alda is great company and so is Christopher Reeve. Either would enhance any show because they're such good talkers. I enjoy the company of extrovert performers far less than people who just sit and talk. Not that I don't admire roaring entertainers, but a talk show requires some give and take, some exchange.

The secret of a sparkling talk show lies in the combination of guests. I suppose the general aim is to get a huge Hollywood star, a singer, and perhaps a home-grown character, but it rarely works out like that and sometimes the most unlikely combination can really work. Sometimes, of course, you don't have much say in the matter anyway. People have pulled out of the show with just hours to go, and then it's not a question of who would go best with the other guests, it's a case of 'Who's free?' In moments of crisis like that you reach for the old dependables. The late and sadly missed Roy Kinnear and Kenneth Williams would always help you out at a moment's notice, and not only that, they'd come up with a great performance. Su Pollard is good fun, and so is Jackie Collins – I'm very fond of her and I like the way she talks. They're bankers, if you like. You know that if they can do it for you, they will, and you know that when they're on screen, they'll do their damndest to make it all work. But although it can be very frustrating when you've done your homework and somebody pulls out, it doesn't alarm me. Yes, it's disappointing, but when someone comes in at the last minute then the adrenalin flows and you can have a very lively show.

One of the most interesting line-ups we had consisted of Judi Dench, Alan Bates and Michael Hordern. It was slightly dangerous to have three actors – they might have almost cancelled one another out, and become so modest and self-effacing and aware of each other's talent that it could all have come to nothing, but Alan Bates is famous for not wanting to do talk shows, and I think he felt that with the other two there, there was safety in numbers. Judi Dench was a dream, so forthcoming and witty. There was an obvious theme to the programme that week, but the following show we had Norman Tebbit, John Cleese and Julio Iglesias – and it's hard to imagine a stranger mixture of people. Still, it worked, and that's all that matters.

Getting Sting and Dustin Hoffman together was inspired. They had met once while on holiday, and not only was Dustin Hoffman a great fan of Sting, but he had written a song which they performed together. To see Dustin Hoffman playing his own song on the piano, and looking up adoringly as Sting sang – well, you don't get many moments like that.

Of course, all the research in the world doesn't mean there won't be a few surprises. We did a show with Sigourney Weaver, Robert Kilroy Silk and Julian Clary. Sigourney was coming on last and we were going to move the seats around during the interval because we felt that she might not be able to concentrate sitting next to the heavily made-up and highly camp Julian. Instead, a message came through during the first part of the show that Sigourney loved Julian, and was asking specifically to be seated next to him. They got on like a house on fire and didn't stop talking afterwards – it was Julian and Robert who wound each other up. It's particularly nice when you can get people together who've always wanted to meet. George Michael was on with Jacqueline Bisset and he confessed that she had been his pin-up and he'd loved her from afar for years.

Yoko Ono, John Cleese and Boy George made a great combination. Boy George was desperate to meet Yoko, he would have done almost anything to be on with her, and Yoko liked the idea of meeting John Cleese because John Lennon had been such a Monty Python fan. Then there was Leslie Crowther, Tom Jones and Julie Andrews – Leslie was totally smitten by Julie Andrews and was thrilled to be on the show with her, Tom Jones is always good fun whatever the combination. He really enjoys himself and will happily stay on afterwards for drinks. He genuinely wants to talk to everybody.

One of my favourite combinations consisted of Patrick Moore, Alan Coren and Zsa Zsa Gabor. Patrick, the lifelong bachelor whose main interests are astronomy, cricket and military marches, next to Zsa Zsa Gabor! From time to time, Patrick would come out with a forthright remark about something we weren't actually discussing. Zsa Zsa was enchanting – whatever I said to her, she'd just giggle and become even more indiscreet. And in the middle of all that was the wit of Alan Coren. It was a good show. All the ingredients were there, and it just took off – I was never quite sure where it was all going, and that's just how it should be.

I don't have any rules about what I ask guests, or any interviewing 'technique'. The idea is really simply to relax people. As David Frost said, 'sometimes the most powerful men in the world can be really nervous of an interview, and sometimes it helps just to throw in a question to keep people quiet at the beginning. Only you have to get the question right. David remembers talking to Issac Asimov, the science-fiction writer, about God and so on. When he asked: 'Is there a force that we don't know about?' Asimov replied 'Well, there may be, but if there is we don't know about it!'

I just try to make sure I look at the person I'm talking to, and show them I'm interested. You've got to be interested. As it happens I usually am. I'm fascinated by writers, as intrigued as anyone by film stars, and genuinely curious about people in politics. A few people make the mistake of thinking that just because we have a politician on the programme, they're going to see *Weekend World*, but that's not our brief. The idea is to present politicians as human beings – not always an easy job – and to offer a few insights into the person behind the tub-thumping

One thing that doing the talk show has taught me is that people hear what they expect to hear. When Margaret Thatcher came on the show my nephew said to me, 'You're not really welcome in this house after having THAT woman on the show.' I said, 'Did you hear me giving her a puff as far as her policies were concerned? Do you remember us talking about politics at any point?' It was simply a profile of someone in office. In fact there was a lovely moment after that show. Barry Manilow was on that same programme and afterwards Mrs Thatcher rushed up to him, got hold of his extremely expensive collar and said, 'You know, this isn't very well made, the shape's all wrong, you should go to someone in Jermyn Street, young man, they'll sort your shirts out for you.' Barry took it very well. He just smiled and shouted, 'Send for my tailor!' Having sorted out Barry's clothes, she then went home to sort out the miners' strike.

Oddly enough, before the show Mrs Thatcher was distinctly nervous – or frit, as she would say. As she stood in the wings, she whispered to her daughter Carol, 'What am I doing here?' But the moment she stepped on, she was herself again, even though it was all quite alien to her.

"It's an emergency government image meeting!"

Cartoon from the *Evening Standard* after Mrs Thatcher appeared on *Aspel & Co.*

Later on, we had Neil Kinnock on the show. He was talking about his childhood in Wales and how he had once wanted to be a detective. Remembering the Welsh love of nicknames, I said, 'Then you'd have been Neil the Squeal.' I'm not sure he liked it much, because there's always the possibility of a label like that sticking. I did the same thing, but on a different show, to Paddy Ashdown, the leader of the Social and Liberal Democrats. He was a guest on *This is Your Life*, and I introduced him first as Peggy Ashdown, and then had to concentrate hard in case I called him Paddy Ashcroft. . . . I thought he might be called Peggy in the House for ever after.

It may be a consolation for them to know that I've been at the receiving end myself. John Timpson once closed the *Today* programme on Radio 4 by saying, 'That's all for today, Mike Aspel will be here tomorrow.' A few days later he had a letter from a listener asking him why he'd told them that his gas bill was arriving the following day. And Kenny Everett, who used to host the programme before mine when I was doing *Family Favourites* on Radio Two, was forever sending me up with his impersonation of Michael Aspirin – or was it Mike Collapsible? The only thing I can say is that at least my mistakes are genuine.

Talk show hosts can also be on the receiving end of questions. I've been the guest of Michael Parkinson, Russell Harty, Des O'Connor, and Gay Byrne on *The Late Late Show* in Dublin. He's been going even longer than Johnny Carson and appearing on his show is a pleasurable experience, with great Irish hospitality thrown in.

I also discovered that being a guest on a talk show is pretty nerve-racking. Yes, there's the relief of knowing you don't have to worry about where the next question is coming from, but that's simply replaced by the worry of where the first answer is coming from. However, it can be fun. These days I think I'd be a useful regular guest. I know what's wanted and I'd do my best to deliver it. As long as I had a sympathetic host, of course.

Somebody, an entertainer himself, once said to me that his idea of a perfect talk show host was someone you don't remember seeing at the end of the programme. I don't go along with that, and not just as a matter of personal pride. You've got to have some status, you've got to have some sort of relationship, however short-lived. Yes, it's a spotlight for the guest, and yes, it's their show to a certain extent, but you can't hope to have a rapport if you don't exist.

COUNTDOWN

We hope that when you're at home watching the show it all looks like a relaxed, late evening chat – at least, that's how it's meant to come across. But of course it's not that simple. In fact nothing's simple about *Aspel and Company*. For a start, there's a whole team of people who work to make sure it happens in the first place. I won't go into too much detail – I remember Glenda Jackson talking about a theatre review she'd read where every single member of the cast was listed – and at the very end it said: 'And Miss Yvonne Smith made a very good prompt . . .' I'll try to spare you that, but I guess it's about time I came clean and admitted it's by no means a one-man show.

There's the producer, the associate producer, the director, the production assistant who works with the director, and the team of researchers. There are the cameramen, the floor managers, the set designer . . . and indeed there is a lady with a prompting machine – in short, a lot of skilled people all dedicated to making the show run smoothly.

On the day of the studio there's usually a good atmosphere in the office. It's tense, but it's fun, too, and once we have all the guests safely at our South Bank studios, we can really start to breathe easily. A car picks them up from wherever they're staying and there's usually a phone, so they can ring us up if they get stuck in traffic jams, or if there is a last-minute change of plan.

In the afternoon, we have a rehearsal, but without the guests. I just walk through the basic moves so the cameras can plot where everybody's going to be, and we try to work out how long people will take to walk down the stairs so we can play the right amount of music. If they can make it, we like the guests to arrive before the audience starts to go in, so they can walk through it, too. Those steps down to the set can be daunting – I think it's everybody's nightmare, stepping out and falling flat on your face. Dusty Springfield was wearing new shoes, with very high heels, and was terrified that she'd slip, so just before she was due to go on, one of the team was dispatched to look for some scissors to scratch the soles with. Oh, the glamour of it all.

It's very rare that anybody arrives alone – Mrs Thatcher brought her daughter Carol, Paul McCartney came with his wife, Linda. A lot of people bring their mums. Fiona Fullerton and Maureen Lipman both had their mothers with them. Emily Lloyd really made an outing out of it and brought her whole family – her mother, grandmother, brother, sister . . .

The researchers meet the guests first, and generally look after them from the time they arrive to the time they leave. It can get a bit like MI5 at times – each guest has his or her own dressing-room with a secret code number to get in – we're constantly changing the numbers so that nobody can sneak in. It got even more complicated when Mrs Thatcher came. It was in the middle of the miners' strike, and feelings were running high. We had to make absolutely sure that her dressing-room number was kept secret, and tracker dogs checked for explosives before she arrived. We even had a hot line set up between the reception at London Weekend and Number 10, and a call did come through, but thankfully it was after we'd done the show, when she was having a drink in the hospitality room.

We expected to have security problems with Mrs Thatcher, but in fact they were nothing compared with those posed by the other guest on that show – Barry Manilow. There were hundreds of screaming women outside and we had to whisk him down to the underground car park and shut the gates behind him.

Once the guests are in, we'll give them a bite to eat or a drink – whatever they want, within reason. Sometimes they'll want some sandwiches and fruit in their dressing-room, others will pop down to the canteen and grab a meal. Tony Curtis wanted sausages, beans and mash and so he queued up with everyone else. He'd been working and playing pretty hard since he'd arrived in London though, and after eating he felt so tired that he wouldn't get dressed. A researcher kept popping in, saying, 'Please, Mr Curtis, you're on soon,' and Tony would say, 'But I'm so tired.' Ten minutes later, he'd still be in his underpants. He was fully dressed for the recording. In fact he wore his hat as well.

When Jim Belushi came, he wanted a particular American brand of beer and we had to search far and wide to find a few cans. We managed that time, but sometimes they've wanted things that we just can't get hold of.

Dennis Waterman felt like going to the canteen so we took him down, got all the food to the check-out, and then discovered that nobody had any money!

We always try to give people an idea of what to wear before they arrive – or rather, of what not to wear. Most people who are used to working with cameras will know that certain colours just don't work, but a few like to be reminded. White, for example, can blur on television. Stripes can go a bit fuzzy, too, and most people bring along a selection of clothes. Hats aren't a great idea – they make life very difficult for the cameraman because you can't see the face underneath (which in some cases might be an advantage). But Pamela Stephenson wanted to wear one of those novelty hats with a hand holding a hammer stuck on it, and Tony Curtis fancied a huge fedora. They had their way. I stuck to my usual balaclava.

Sometimes people's clothes give you problems that you just couldn't have imagined. When Phil Collins came on, his jacket had such wide shoulders that I had to lean to one side to see the monitor TV set which the producer uses to scribble messages to me.

I usually follow fashion very slowly and creep in just as it starts to look dated, but then I think that's the way I should do it. There's no point in me appearing with a pig-tail and diamanté donkey jacket. Apart from looking ridiculous I'd feel uncomfortable, and if you feel uncomfortable, you do a rotten show. So I'm put into the hands of what used to be called 'Wardrobe' but now has the grander title of 'Costume Designers', who are keen for me to join the twentieth century sartorially, which would involve climbing into one of those colossal suits. I resist for two good reasons – a) they don't suit me, and b) I'm the wrong age for them. I've stepped into some of those trousers and disappeared among the pleats. When I sit down they billow up in front of me and I look as if I've got a water melon under there. So I end up being pretty conservative about what I wear and draw the line at a discreet pleat here and there, usually around the chin. The aim is to have about three suits per series – I certainly don't want to come prancing on every week in something different, but neither do I want people to groan when they see me in the same old suit. All that fuss, and all that's wanted is for nobody to notice my clothes at all.

My favourite line on the subject came from Michael Grade, who studied the jacket being worn by one of his trendier producers. It was like an attack of migraine, all zig-zags and blobs. 'If you had an outdoor aerial,' said Michael, 'you could get rid of all that.'

Most people have a dab of make-up before they go on, reluctant though some are. You tend to look a little washed out under the lights without something. A lot of people apply their own – Joan Collins was one. Zsa Zsa Gabor brought her own hairdresser. Sometimes the guests meet up while they're having their make-up done and it's a great ice-breaker, sitting there together with your hair scraped back and having your face powdered.

Before the show we have a little reception in hospitality, and if I meet the guests at all before the show, it'll either be in make-up or there, over a glass of orange juice. It's certainly never anything stronger than that, for me at any rate, but the guests can have what they like. I'd rather not talk to the guests much beforehand simply because I find it works better just to say hello, and thanks for coming, and leave it at that. The last thing you want is to start an involved conversation because when you come to do it for real, it can all seem a bit stale. Also, it could give my guests time to go off the whole idea.

About ten minutes before the show begins, the audience is seated – not too comfortably, we like them to stay awake. On the set itself we've had, more or less, a different arrangement for every series. First we had the idea of a desk, but I'm not supposed to be a bank manager. On the other hand, I could put all my notes on it, and it would be somewhere to rest the elbows. Johnny Carson in America always looks comfortable and authoritative behind a desk, and in a way I was sorry we abandoned that idea.

For the first series, we had little sit-up chairs on which we perched and swivelled, but then we were still experimenting. In those days, too, when the guests entered they crossed between me and the cameras, which did strange things to the perspective. This was particularly obvious when people like Clint Eastwood and Charlton Heston came on. The difference between our heights, which was already sizeable, was exaggerated even more, and letters began to arrive asking, 'Is Aspel a midget?' It's silly things like that which get in the way of the actual show, so for the next series, I suggested a couch, low enough for me to put my arm over the back of it, but high enough to stop me sliding off on to the floor. Mel Smith has been on the opening show of two series so far, and it was the first thing he mentioned. 'So glad to see you've got a new sofa. The last time I came on, it looked like the corner of a pub – it's more like a Sloane Square wine bar now, very comfy,' he said. What we've got now, I suppose, is rather a curious set – chat in the round. It was designed to make the audience part of the show. The chairs are in the middle of the set, and the audience sits all around us, which may be a bit disconcerting for the people who've come to see their heroes, and spend the evening studying the backs of their necks. The chairs we have now were actually designed with our chat show in mind, not so low that knees come up to chins and reveal too much sock, nor so wide as to encourage fidgeting, with an upright back to prevent slouching, and arm rests to give the nervous something to grip.

After all that, one of the arms fell off recently, reminding me of the time the same thing happened during a recording of *Give Us A Clue*. In fact, due to a fault in assembly all the arms came off all the chairs. I should have seized the opportunity and said to Una Stubbs, 'Here's your next title, *A Farewell to Arms*.'

The first five series featured Ken Jones, a band leader who also composed the show's theme music. He played the guests on and off and also accompanied the people who sang – Paul McCartney, Liza Minnelli and Tom Jones, and a few more unlikely names, too, such as Lenny Henry, George Segal on the banjo, and Patrick Moore on the xylophone. He coped with whatever was thrown at him. For instance, when Oliver Reed made his now famous appearance with slightly more than a little Dutch courage inside him, he suddenly took it into his head that he wanted to sing. Completely unexpectedly, he stood up and said, 'I'm going to sing a Keith Richards song' and just launched into it. The only person more surprised than me was Ken, who just had to follow along as best he could.

When Les Dawson was a guest on the show, we discovered that he and Ken had been at school together, and Les could not resist reminding him of those happy days: 'The school we went to was so poor, if you put your hand up they thought it was a hold up. Ken and I both went to music lessons and the first interest I ever had in music was the teacher at the school. She was playing the piano and I stood there transfixed, a little kid with a pin through his jersey from the slums. And she said, 'Schubert –' I said, 'No, I smelt it when I came in.' Do you know, Ken, you've never changed . . .'

'Really?' said Ken.

'You still look a mess,' said Les.

Sadly, Ken died in the spring of 1988 while on a ski-ing holiday. His last words would have made a fine song title. Half-way down a mountain he turned to his wife, Ruth. 'Haven't we come a long way?' he said, and collapsed.

Ken was a great character, and so is Bill Martin. Before each show is recorded, the warm-up man will go out and do just that − 'warm up' the audience. We always have Bill, who is the best. He'll go out, tell a few jokes and get people in a responsive mood. Bill used to be half of a double act with Dave Allen. He knows how to make people laugh, without whipping them into such a state of excitement that they feel a keen sense of anti-climax when the host of the show comes on. We don't hold up placards telling the audience what to do. Years ago they were instructed every inch of the way with placards reading 'Applaud', 'Laugh', and 'Go home!'

The most tense part of the show is, of course, just before the guests come on. Hopefully, everyone is ready, sitting in the Green Room behind the set, and then the music plays and on I go. I've had a series of producers, all with very different personalities. One used to slap me on the back and say 'Get out there, son, and do it', another would pluck at my sleeve and murmur, 'Don't forget the one-liners . . .' Now, you just can't plan one-liners. You simply open your mouth and hope something comes out and you can only do that if you're relaxed. Nothing destroys a sense of humour more than fear. Nothing activates the bladder as much as fear, either, and this is the moment when the studio audience will often hear the clatter of heels across the floor as guests make a last-minute dash for the loo.

As soon as they're installed in the Green Room, guests are looked after by the Floor Manager. He'll take them to the top of the stairs and make sure they know when to go on − usually by the gracious means of a prod in the back. The music starts, the guest walks down the stairs, we shake hands − and we're off.

MAGIC MOMENTS

There have been a few moments during the making of *Aspel and Company* which have aged me considerably – but then I comfort myself with the thought that life would be very dull without any crises to get the heart racing. Mostly, crises arise when a guest pulls out at the last minute and we're urgently looking for a replacement – sometimes we've had just a matter of hours. Occasionally, it just looks as though someone's not going to turn up because for one reason or another they've been held up. A few are just plain awkward and play the game of holding you to ransom. Others try to demand their fee up front. A difficult moment for me occurred when Phil Collins came on the show, simply because what I knew but he didn't, was that he was going to be my first guest on *This Is Your Life* the following week. I was desperately trying not to let the cat out of the bag, and a few tricky moments came about just because of a few crossed wires.

That's what happened when we had Mrs Thatcher and Barry Manilow on the same show. When we originally talked to Barry about it, we already knew that the Prime Minister would be guest that night, so we told him all about it, and he had this great idea. 'I'd like to sing with Mrs Thatcher,' he said. 'Interesting thought,' we all said, 'we'll talk about that later.' Negotiations went ahead but it all got a bit bizarre because at the time Barry's manager was called Larry, his road manager was called Gary and his assistant was called Harry – so we had Barry, Larry, Gary and Harry – in fact, I think there were two Gary's, just to make it confusing.

Anyway, at midnight two nights before the show, the director, Nick, is sitting at home when the phone rings. 'Hi Nick, it's Gary. We're at Los Angeles airport and we're just about to leave but

Barry's a little unsure about the song.' 'Which song?' asked Nick nervously. 'The song with Mrs Thatcher,' said Gary brightly. 'We were told that it was going to be arranged for Barry to sing "The White Cliffs of Dover" with Mrs Thatcher at the end of the show. And the thing is, that Barry doesn't really want to get on the plane until it's all sorted out. So Larry's going to stay in the car with Barry, and Harry and Gary . . .' Now, by this point Nick wasn't sure if it was all some ghastly joke or not, and then he realized what had happened. Eventually he said, 'OK, we'll call Number 10 tomorrow . . .' but mercifully the idea was abandoned and we were spared. I don't know though, it would have made great television.

A similar thing happened with Mel Brooks, only in reverse. He decided he wanted to do a number on the show, and then knock the piano and the orchestra into bits – destroy the whole lot. So the night before the show, the carpenters at London Weekend were working all hours, making a collapsible piano and orchestra. The next day Mel came in and said, 'Actually, I don't think it's such a great idea . . .' We said, 'YES, IT'S A VERY GOOD IDEA!' And in the end the demolition went ahead.

At least both of those incidents had humour – life can get pretty tedious when it's missing and it was very definitely absent the night Richard Gere was a guest. Here's a man who's very good-looking, whose very name is enough to get women in an audience squealing with delight but who can't bear the thought of being a sex symbol. The whole thing about a talk show is that you have to ask the questions that people are interested in – not in a way that puts the guest on the spot or makes them feel awkward – we're not out to 'get' anyone, that's not the idea of it at all – but certain things must be asked. If the guest doesn't want to answer, that's up to him or her. But Richard Gere took exception to the questions even being asked. He even took exception to the introduction I gave him and when it came to the commercial break, he wagged his finger at me. After the show he yelled at the researcher, 'You betrayed me – you broke our word, you promised we wouldn't talk about sex symbols,' and left the building. And yet that part of the interview could have been dismissed with a laugh in five seconds. He had plugged his new film, discussed his talented family, talked about his work in the theatre, and we had listened attentively while he outlined his search for spiritual enlightenment and concern about the problems in Tibet. He feels very strongly about the atrocities being perpetrated there and indeed gave his appearance fee to the Tibet charity which he supports. What he didn't do was relax and enjoy himself.

When someone decides to take offence and be uncooperative during a show it can have a nasty effect on the atmosphere. Everything goes very cold. There's a kind of silence which has nothing to do with paying attention, it's all to do with people wishing they were somewhere else – and I'm referring to the audience.

I have had guests who have been speechless, monosyllabic, obtuse and recalcitrant, but more often because of nerves or discomfort than deliberately so. People are rarely so rude that you can say, 'Look, we're not enjoying this, are we? Let's call it a day.' Nerves can play havoc with someone's ability to tell a good story. And it can get awkward when people take things too literally – you say, 'Hello, how are you?' and twenty minutes later you're still listening to their philosophy of life. That happened with one American actress whose very name now depresses me. Every time I tried to change the subject, she'd close her eyes, hold up her hand and say, 'I haven't finished yet.' I thought, 'I wish you bloody well would . . .'

Usually though, our crises are more to do with logistics. The day that Seb Coe was a guest, he was opening a spinal injuries unit in a hospital in Birmingham. We had organized a helicopter to get him down to London in time. The only thing that could have stopped us was fog. That day it was foggy. So the researcher went to Birmingham to meet him and all the time he was talking to the patients, she was thinking, 'We've got to go!' There was a car waiting, but because of the fog they abandoned the idea of driving down and went to the railway station, caught a train with minutes to spare, picked up the car that was waiting for them the other end, rang the studio from the car phone to let them know where they were, and ran into London Weekend Television. The first guest, Victoria Wood, was already on, and Seb had to puff his way on immediately. I read in a newspaper recently that he'd said, 'I've only ever done one chat show and I'll never do another one.' Probably because of that, but he was really very good and I'm sure he doesn't mean it. Do you Seb? Seb?

Sometimes it seems that the problems are completely out of our control. The second time that Yoko Ono came on the show, it was to talk about Albert Goldman's book on John Lennon. In fact, she dismissed it with one word – 'rubbish' – but we'd just started the show when there was a loud bang. There was a firework display going on outside but it did sound very much like a gun, and Yoko absolutely froze. She was obviously shaken, and who could blame her after what she's been through.

The night that George Harrison and Ringo Starr came on, it really did seem as though there was some mischief afoot. They were talking, very movingly, about John Lennon's death, and about how Ringo had been aware of John's presence since. Whether he was around that night or not we'll never know, but it seemed that everything that could go amiss, did. Cameras went wrong, George's microphone wasn't working and we had to start the show again, a light exploded. It was easy to believe that someone, somewhere, was playing games with us.

We had problems with spirits of a different nature the night Oliver Reed joined us. I heard some uncertain footsteps and he lurched on, waving a jug of orange juice, which was not the drink he had obviously been consuming in huge quantities. He was so rip-roaring drunk, in fact, that he made newspaper headlines the next day. The front page of *The Sun* carried a picture of him, mouth wide open, eyes rolling. Apparently a lot of people were outraged, and the switchboard jammed, but as one critic pointed out, it would have been more extraordinary if he had behaved like a bank manager. I was aware during the encounter that it was very compelling viewing. All I didn't want to happen was for him to become violent, which I didn't think was ever on the cards. I was more worried that he might fall over and hurt himself.

Now, when I say hello to the audience before we begin recording the show, I point to the chairs, and say: 'Elizabeth Taylor sat here, and Michael Caine sat here, and Oliver Reed was all along there . . .'

Another guest who kept the switchboard operators busy was Dave Allen. He's a great observer of human nature, and the story that caused all the trouble was this. (If it upset you the first time, please move on to the next paragraph.) 'I like the word fart,' said Dave. 'I think it's a good word because it describes what it is. I mean, if somebody comes up to you and says, "I had a touch of flatulence," you think, "You farted." My grandmother used to say, "Whose bottom coughed?" But the funniest expression I ever heard was in New Zealand where I was staying with friends of mine and their young daughter. Now, she was walking across the room when she farted, and her father said, "Did you whisper?" Whisper was his

Time between takes for a
Bugs Bunny impersonation.
(This is the *real* Aspel,
under the make-up.)

Sting sings Dustin's song.

The encounter with Clint Eastwood that prompted the letters
asking if Aspel was a midget...

...Dudley Moore assuring me I'm not!

euphemism for fart. But I thought to myself, one day somebody is going to say to the child, "Come and whisper in my ear . . ."'

Apparently hundreds of viewers took offence at that – but thousands more are still chuckling.

At least when a guest is misbehaving they're where we expect them to be. The real problems can arise when they just don't turn up. Sometimes it's all a 'star' ploy. One American comedienne threatened to pull out with just one hour to go. I don't know, maybe that's just the way it's done over there. Her representative rang and said she wasn't coming on. Simple as that. And then put the phone down, and waited for us to ring back to find out what she was demanding. She wanted everything changed. She wanted to go on and talk to the audience before the show began: 'Like me, please like me,' she said to them, which is an approach not appreciated by British audiences. She also wanted to go on first, not last. We helped her with her problem because it meant she relaxed and gave a better 'performance'. Needless to say though she left the

'This is nothing – wait until you see the hospitality room!'

studio offering no apologies, no thanks, no farewells. It's true that the show has to go on but if such behaviour caught on I'd be bound to go on and say, 'Ladies and gentlemen, so-and-so isn't coming' because they not only want to appear on the show, they want to produce it as well!'

Sometimes it's nobody's fault at all. Richard Dreyfuss was booked one week and on the night of the show a confusion over dates and times led his film company to arrange a business call that linked up Los Angeles, London, Australia and New York and he just had to be there. He was sitting in the Savoy, only two hundred yards from the studio – we could almost see him. That's why we never celebrate anything until it's happened. At times like that, you call on your mates, and Kenny Everett kindly got us out of a spot of trouble there and agreed to come on at short notice.

So you can see we've had our share of tricky moments. Another one was when Tony Curtis ended the show himself, long before we were ready. He just stood up, said, 'With that, I bid you goodnight,' waved his arms and left. Luckily by then we had enough material – together with a few more worry lines.

My favourite put-down of all came from Chuck Berry. As he got up to go to the microphone, I asked him what he was going to sing. 'Small fee, small hit,' he said. And there's really no answer to that.

Of course, there have been just as many happy moments making *Aspel and Company* as crises – the trouble is that they tend not to make such good stories!

Many of the best ones arise out of the preparations for the show and so are never shared by the viewers. The researchers have had some interesting experiences when they've been out and about – it's not all work and no play – just mostly. Like the time that Clint Eastwood was being interviewed by a researcher in Paris. They finished chatting in the afternoon, and the researcher went back to her hotel room. A little while later the phone rang. The caller said, 'Mr Eastwood would like to know if you're on your own this evening, and if you are, would you like to join him for dinner?' It was all quite innocent, he was genuinely worried that she was on her own. And of course she accepted.

It's agreeable to know that although star temperaments certainly do exist, there are just as many nice people as awkward ones. Tony Curtis has a certain modesty. We were to meet him at the airport, and when we were making all the arrangements with him on the phone, he said, 'Are you sure you'll be able to recognize me?' He arrived, wearing a dazzling white suit and a huge hat, just to make sure.

Peter Ustinov was being interviewed in Geneva – in fact that interview was conducted in fluent German by Peter and the researcher. After all, why talk in English when you can give yourself a little challenge? Afterwards they went shopping together and she helped him choose some shoes for his wife. On the summer's day that Michael Caine was being interviewed, he and the researcher sat and watched Wimbledon on the telly together for an hour or so before they got down to work.

Not all guests accept an invitation immediately. It's often the result of months of chasing, and is very satisfying when that person is particularly famous, impossibly busy, or known to dislike talk shows. Elizabeth Taylor, Margaret Thatcher and Clint Eastwood would all fit neatly into that line up. Anita Dobson decided to come on our show and announce that she was leaving *EastEnders*. That was quite a coup, considering that *EastEnders* is a BBC programme.

Chuck Berry and Dustin Hoffman were feathers in our cap, and so was Harrison Ford, who is known for being 'a very private person' as they say in Los Angeles. Actually he simply likes to live a normal life and keeps himself to himself, but in the end he decided that he would do it. He was on with Mel Smith, who had done a beer commercial in which he sent up Indiana Jones – Ford's most famous role. We showed Harrison Ford this advert on the show. He threw back his head and roared with laughter. Afterwards, the representative from the film company said, 'I've been looking after him for two weeks and that's the first time I've seen his teeth . . .' I asked him if he would like a video of the show and he said, 'No thanks, the experience was enough.' He was still smiling – just.

I relished the moment during a rehearsal once when Mel Brooks suddenly boomed at the researcher, 'Judith – go to my dressing-room and put on that thing I bought you!' And the time that Dame Edna came on, kissed Claire Rayner firmly on each cheek and left her with two luscious pink lip prints for the rest of the show. One of my favourite moments was when Nigel Havers was a guest. He's a gem, always full of good humour, and he's been on a few times, now, but this particular moment was when I noticed in the studio lights a glint of trouser zip. I thought, 'I've just got to say something, and if it doesn't go down too well, we can edit it out afterwards'. I said, 'You know I've rarely said this to anyone in real life and certainly never on television, but Nigel, your flies are undone.' He was almost relieved – for one ghastly moment, he'd thought that I was going to tell him I loved him.

I enjoyed the whole of the Chuck Berry interview – I only wish we'd had longer. He played a song at the end of the interview, and all he said to the band was: 'When I kick, that means I'm going to start, and when I kick my leg again, that means I'm going to stop.' That's all they had to go on – they didn't even know what key they were meant to be playing in. I don't know how they felt about it, but the rest of us loved it.

THE ELIZABETH TAYLOR EXPERIENCE

Ah, Elizabeth – what memories I have of that show. From my point of view it was a complete success – fun, interesting and the chance for me to meet someone whom I'd admired from afar since I was 14 years old. One critic wrote of the show: 'Of course it's great to see her but why was it necessary to have such a fawning and sycophantic performance?' I think that's very unfair – Elizabeth was just pleased to see me.

Surprisingly I wasn't at all nervous that evening. I was pretty certain of the approach I had to take and the fact that we're virtually the same age was an advantage. I don't think the interview would have been so good with a younger man. And Elizabeth knew that I knew all about her, and she also knew that she was the only person I'd ever written to for a photograph. I was fourteen then, I'd seen her in *National Velvet*, and had been barmy about her ever since.

So the ammunition was there, the time was right and I think she enjoyed herself. She gives you 'The Look' in much the same way that Lauren Bacall does, and you play the game – Michael Parkinson set the rules with Shirley MacLaine. So people may say that we're flirting. That's one word for it. Coaxing is another and sycophancy is another – you put your own interpretation on it but if it gets a good show, then it's all a matter of semantics.

Elizabeth agreed to do our programme after we'd spent five years gently hammering at her representatives – and of course we weren't the only people after her, the whole world was beating at her door. But it turned in our favour and persistence paid off. It would be nice to think that she woke up one day and thought, 'I've got to do

Michael's show.' What probably happened was that she suddenly decided the time was right for her to do some publicity and she had something to talk about, her book, *Elizabeth Takes Off*.

She was also, I suppose, very pleased with the way she was looking, and rightly so. In addition, she knew that ours was the kind of show which would give her the right sort of outlet.

But of course nothing's ever that straightforward, and we had our share of hiccups along the way. Elizabeth said yes, she would do it, but that she didn't want an audience, she just wanted to record it with me. Then she changed her mind and said she'd have an audience after all, and then, best of all, she said not only would she have an audience, but she'd like them to ask her questions. That was completely her own idea and it worked brilliantly.

The audience turned out to be very efficient interviewers – I got quite depressed. It sparked off some very good discussions, far more than we had time to transmit.

Now obviously Elizabeth Taylor can demand her own terms – she's one of the biggest stars in the world and she could easily have been a prima donna. In fact she didn't demand anything, apart from a dressing-room on the ground floor because she was having great difficulty with her back at the time, and being in pain, was using a wheelchair most of the time. Unfortunately, television studios are strangely designed and dressing-rooms are often miles away from the studio, so we had to find a place where she and her entourage could relax in comfort without the need to climb stairs. The only thing on the ground floor that was similar to a dressing-room was a gents' loo, so we set about disguising its true purpose by dressing it up for the evening. A researcher found out her favourite colour – a sort of purply-pink and we laid on her favourite drink – Perrier water with cranberry juice.

I had a feeling I was going to enjoy that show, right from the moment Elizabeth walked on to the set. All the guests have to be wired up with a radio mike, and just before she went on, she said: 'I've got this thing strapped between my legs – I hope it doesn't give way ...' I introduced her, she took two steps, and there was an almighty clatter. The mike had given way and was trailing between her feet. The laugh she gave was *so* dirty that I knew it was going to be all right. From that moment, everybody relaxed.

In the end the show went on far longer than we expected and was fairly raunchy. Now, for the benefit of anyone who missed it, here is the whole, unexpurgated version.

Michael Aspel:	I've only once in my life written a fan letter to a film star. I was fourteen at the time, so was she; she sent me a signed photograph which I kept in the breast pocket of my school blazer until both photograph and blazer fell apart. Since then there have been other men in her life but tonight, the plans I laid all those years ago reach fruition as I proudly introduce my partner for the evening. Ladies and gentlemen – Elizabeth Taylor ... Well, if it's all right with you, for the first seven hours can I just look at you?
Elizabeth Taylor:	I must say you look very good for your age.
Michael:	You were listening. I should really say 'Welcome home' because you are British-born, aren't you?
Elizabeth:	Yes. I still have a British passport.
Michael:	How long did you actually live here as a child?
Elizabeth:	I left when I was about eight.
Michael:	But you still feel British?
Elizabeth:	Yes, I'm half and half.
Michael:	Now, you're looking slim and lovely but, as the world knows, there was a time when you weren't quite as sylph-like?
Elizabeth:	I was the great white whale.
Michael:	We have in fact a picture here which I'm sure you won't mind us seeing, because of the context of your present appearance.
Elizabeth:	Isn't that pretty?
Michael:	How long ago was that?
Elizabeth:	About seven years ago.
Michael:	And how much did you weigh?
Elizabeth:	I would say about 185 pounds.
Michael:	What's that, 13 stone or something?
Elizabeth:	That's a boiling piece. You can tell I really cared about my hair and how I looked – I was so together!
Michael:	And how do you feel now, seeing that?
Elizabeth:	I can't believe that I was really that desperate, that I let myself go that completely.

Michael: Do you know why you got that way?

Elizabeth: Obviously, I had a very deep sense of pain and loneliness – that wasn't a happy person.

Michael: But were you always obsessed with food? Was that part of it?

Elizabeth: No, I could eat and get away with it. I was one of those lucky ones. But it was the combination of not doing anything, drinking too much and all my other addictions.

Michael: The comedians and the comics were merciless, weren't they? At the time, you were the butt of some very unkind jokes?

Elizabeth: Oh, some of them got quite rich.

Michael: What was the most unkind one that you can think of?

Elizabeth: There is one rather funny one, I think: 'Elizabeth Taylor was seen in town today wearing a yellow dress, and a group of children at the bus stop went towards her and boarded her.'

Michael: You're laughing bravely, it must have hurt at the time.

Elizabeth: Well, it did and then I laughed the loudest, but it hurt inside.

Michael: So what finally made you actually do something?

Elizabeth: First I did something with my insides. I went to the Betty Ford Centre and cleaned myself up. I was a mess. And I admitted to myself that I was an alcoholic and I had a problem with prescription pills, and in order to survive – in order to live – had to change that. And I *wanted* to live and be a whole, complete human being. I spent about seven weeks there and I felt great inside but it was like I was wearing the wrong slip cover. The outside didn't match the inside and I wanted them all to kind of get together.

Michael: You were *thinking* thin and healthy but the outside didn't match?

Elizabeth: Yes. And my body was lumbersome and sluggish and it slowed me down. So I thought, 'Why not lose the weight?' Look as good on the outside as you feel on the inside?

Michael: This Betty Ford Clinic is a famous place, but what were your first impressions of it?

Elizabeth: One of sheer terror. I guess it was the first time really in my life I'd been totally left on my own. And the first night I arrived there, there was no one even to greet me. They were all in a meeting, and they didn't quite know how to deal with me – I was the first celebrity ever to have gone. And they were wondering whether I should have private classes or be with the group and have group therapy and they decided, yes, she is like everybody else. And of course that was the best way to treat me because we were all there for one reason and that was to get over our addiction and to cure ourselves and be better.

Michael: When you submit yourself to that regime then you are bound to do all they tell you? Is it like that?

Elizabeth: Oh, yes. And part of it is discipline – you know, making your room up and one day you clean the porch, one day you sweep down the kitchen ... you have different duties every day.

Michael: Have you ever done that sort of thing before?

Elizabeth: Well, I'd always been a bit too busy – and clever! I get a maid to come in and do it for me.

Michael: But did you find it humiliating?

Elizabeth: No, not at all, it wasn't meant to be humiliating. We were all there on the same level, we were all there with the same problem. None of us was better off, none of us was worse off – none of us was a better human being or a worse human being.

Michael: But the others not being celebrities, did they find it odd? Did they give you a difficult time?

Elizabeth: Not at all, they were very helpful. Like when I had to carry the garbage out – because of my bad back, the girls helped me with my duty and

	it was all right with the counsellors because of my back – it wasn't special treatment.
Michael:	Is it true that your own children testified, as it were, against you on this?
Elizabeth:	All except Marie, who had just had a baby; and my brother and Roddy McDowall. I don't know if you have family intervention in this country. It's when the family come in and they've been prepared by a doctor whose speciality it is, and they have lists of things that they have witnessed you do, that have embarrassed and humiliated them. They say, 'I love you mum, but I've seen you do this. I've watched you do that. And the reason I'm telling this to you, is because I want you to live.'
Michhael:	And what effect did all this have?
Elizabeth:	Oh, staggering, it leaves you totally speechless. It's so sincere and done with such love that you know it must be agony for them and your one thought is, 'Oh God, how could I have hurt these people like that?'
Michael:	It sounds almost as if it will be too agonizing for them. I can't imagine people in this country putting themselves through that, no matter how much they love that person.
Elizabeth:	It *is* hard for them. And some people in a family intervention turn around and say, 'Bugger off, it's my own life, and I never want to see you again.' So you always take that chance of ruining a relationship ... When I was at the centre, they don't encourage you to stop smoking, stop drinking coffee, or lose weight. They just want you to do the things that you're there for. And after about four months I thought I was strong enough to tackle the weight, and that it wouldn't be too much going on at once. Actually, I had fun inventing my own diet because I had gone on diets before, I'd gone to fat farms, too, but it had never lasted. So I thought, 'Well, I'll devise a diet with the kind of

food I like, because I don't *like* going hungry. I can't bear that feeling of rats gnawing at my stomach. And I think it's unnecessary on a diet to feel unpleasant. So I thought, 'I'll invent a diet where you feel good *and* you can eat.'

Michael: So dieting hasn't now become your new obsession?

Elizabeth: Not an obsession, but I don't want to ever get like that again.

Michael: There are a lot of fat people, of course, who quite like being fat. Is it not possible to be fat *and* happy?

Elizabeth: Oh, I think it is, and I'm not saying that everybody should be slim, in a size 6 or 8. If you're happy in a size 14, that's fine. It's for the people who *aren't* happy with the weight they're at, or if it's unhealthy – if it's endangering your health and you have to do something about it; if you've been told by your doctor to lose weight. It's for people who *want* to lose weight.

Michael: And do you allow yourself the occasional binge?

Elizabeth: I call them pig-outs. My favourite pig-out is that wonderful Southern Fried Chicken, mashed potatoes with dribbling gravy, broad beans and corn on the cob and then some kind of gooey chocolate dessert.

Michael: Mmmmm, you'll make me dribble in a minute. Is all this easy, and does the book explain that it is easy for someone who is not Elizabeth Taylor to achieve this?

Elizabeth: If I can do it, *anybody* can do it!

Michael: And what is the new you like? What effect has this had on you as a person now?

Elizabeth: I feel much more vigorous; more full of life. I think I'm much more open, at ease, and comfortable with life – I find life a big adventure – I'm enjoying it. And there are so many things out there to do . . . and I'm doing them.

Michael: I'll ask you what you're up to soon, but I've got to strap my safety belt for this question. I have to ask, where does all the skin *go*? Has it involved plastic surgery?

Elizabeth: I did have a chin tuck, and the lady who worked on the book with me said, 'Now, Elizabeth, you know we're going to be together for months and we have to be absolutely honest with each other. I've heard all *kinds* of stories . . .' We were out by the pool and she said, 'Now, we don't have to talk about it, but have you had suction, and tucks all over your body?' I said, 'Just a second, Jane,' and I stripped off completely, twirled around for her, and she said: 'Thank you, Elizabeth, you haven't.' Now I'll do that for you here . . . but I'm sure you'll take my word.

Michael: I was just going to say I didn't believe a word of it but . . . Let me ask you then about the good life – you're a single woman again, are you enjoying every minute of that?

Elizabeth: Yes, I am.

Michael: Who are the men in your life?

Elizabeth: They have been different, a few here and there.

Michael: George Hamilton has been a friend for a long time?

Elizabeth: Yes.

Michael: And Malcolm Forbes – now he's a man of advanced years – he is in his seventies . . .

Elizabeth: No, no, he's in his sixties.

Michael: Oh, sorry. He's a mad biker though, is that true?

Elizabeth: Yes, we've gone on wonderful bike races together, and he's a wonderful balloonist. He's very adventurous, a very young man.

Michael: Younger than I thought, certainly! And is marriage number eight on the cards?

Elizabeth: I hope that one day before I die, I'll marry again, but I don't have anybody in mind, no.

Michael: In your book you mentioned the two great loves

Elizabeth: of your life so far, Mike Todd and Richard Burton – what were their special qualities?

Elizabeth: Oh, they are too innumerable to go into, and it's just too personal to go into.

Michael: If Mike Todd had lived, though, do you feel that your life wouldn't have taken any other direction?

Elizabeth: If he had lived, I'm sure we would have stayed together – I'm sure.

Michael: But you met Richard Burton filming *Cleopatra*, as again the world knows. Was the chemistry instantly apparent, as it was to us?

Elizabeth: Well, I had known him on and off for about nine years, and my attitude was resentful – you know, I'm *not* going to be another notch in his gun belt, and all that, was going on. The first day on the set he was hung-over and very vulnerable, and his hands were shaking. He asked me to hold the coffee up to his lips and I was gone. He was so sweet.

Michael: You and Richard Burton had a wildly extravagant lifestyle, planes were exchanged and diamonds ... What is the most extravagant thing you ever did, can you remember?

Elizabeth: Oh Lord, we did so many extravagant things – all sort of at the last minute. Like, we'd be in mid-air, flying from one country to another country, and all of a sudden we'd decide to fly to Venice for lunch. Things like that.

Michael: You were the original hijackers then, were you? Have you found that other women have been jealous of your glorious jewels?

Elizabeth: I don't think so. I think women like to look at them. I like to look at other women wearing pretty jewels – I don't want to grab them off and put them in my pocket ... not frequently, anyhow.

Michael: Do you let them try them on at all?

Elizabeth: Oh yes, that's part of the fun of it.

Michael: What is that monster on your left hand there?

Elizabeth: That's the Krupp diamond.

Michael: And do diamonds increase in value as the years pass, like property?

Elizabeth: Yes, if it's a perfect stone – which this is – they retain their value. But the price of diamonds can fluctuate, like property.

Michael: And what did that one cost?

Elizabeth: Golly, I can't remember what Richard paid for it, actually. But I've been offered several million for it.

Michael: Several million?

Elizabeth: No, I'm not selling.

Michael: Can I just touch it? That's $30,000 I got there. I'm told that Princess Margaret, too, was interested in your jewellery, is that right?

Elizabeth: The first time I wore this, I'd had it for about two months and I was talking to Princess Margaret, but as we spoke, I could see she was following my hand with her eyes. And finally she said, 'That's the most vulgar thing I've ever seen in my life.' But then she asked me if she could try it on.

Michael: You have a little jewellery, don't you – you bought a Windsor piece ... that cost a pretty penny, my dear.

Elizabeth: Yes, but you see that was all right because it was going to the Louis Pasteur Institute for Aids, it's the only piece of important jewellery I've ever bought myself. And I went through *reams* of guilt, but then I thought, 'No, it's all right because it's going for Aids,' and also it has a very sweet, sentimental story behind it.

Michael: Something you could tell us?

Elizabeth: Well, Richard and I knew the Duke and Duchess of Windsor quite well, and spent a lot of time with them in Paris, and this was our favourite piece of jewellery. And actually, one day, because she knew it was my favourite, she said that I could have permission to have it copied and gave me the name of the jeweller, which I thought was so sweet. I never did, but when it came up for auction, it just seemed like it would make her smile, and the money was going to a good cause, too.

Michael: And you could do it, so that's fine. But with all this wildly extravagant lifestyle, you were also expected to sit in pubs after rugby matches and sing bawdy songs. . . .

Elizabeth: Which I adored ... I miss pubs, and the bawdy songs, nothing is as good as English, Welsh or Scottish or Celtic bawdy songs. Why is that?

Michael: It's the richness of the language – that we know more filth than anybody else.

Elizabeth: I'll drink to that!

Michael: Why do you think your relationship with Richard Burton was so fiery – was it temperament or was it just the booze?

Elizabeth: No, I think we were two very volatile people. As a matter of fact we were like two atom bombs – we'd go off together and there would be this tremendous explosion but we'd come down together, too. We didn't sulk and we didn't pout and it never lasted. And we had a *ball* fighting . .

Michael: Worth it for the making up?

Elizabeth: It was always exciting – and we knew it never meant anything.

Michael: Do you think he wasted his life and his talent?

Elizabeth: No, I don't, and I get very cross when people say that he wasted his talent. Just because he went to Hollywood and was paid a lot of money doesn't mean he was wasting his talent. He did some remarkable performances. He was superb in *Anne of a Thousand Days, Becket, Who's Afraid of Virginia Woolf, The Spy Who Came in From The Cold, Where Eagles Dare* – they've been innumerable. He was nominated for an Oscar eight times – not many actors have achieved that.

Michael: But how did he rationalize doing the rubbish?

Elizabeth: Money.

Michael: That explains it. Do you think the Betty Ford Clinic would have helped him, and did he ever get tempted?

Elizabeth: I don't know – the last time I saw him he was very curious about it, he was very proud of what I had done. And he asked me a lot of very pertinent questions which seemed to me more than idle curiosity. I think he was, perhaps, interested.

Michael: You're very much involved with working for Aids research, what is the name of the organization that you're the chairwoman of?

Elizabeth: AMFAR. The American Foundation For Aids Research.

Michael: And did you get involved in this for very special reasons?

Elizabeth: No, I was simply asked to be General Chairman of the first dinner to raise funds for Aids. It was in Los Angeles and it was murderously difficult – no one wanted to be involved, no one wanted to talk about it, no one wanted to lend their names; no one wanted to come and entertain, no one wanted to buy a ticket. There was this terrible stigma – it was like, 'It's their problem, let them handle it,' with 'they' meaning the homosexual community. There would have *been* no Hollywood without the homosexual community, and just as human beings, I felt we owed our fellow man a certain responsibility. I became really angry at this very obvious silence. No one was doing anything· and I thought, 'Well, hell, I'm guilty of doing exactly the same thing as everybody else is doing. And I'm angry that I'm not doing anything,' so I thought maybe for once I could use my name – my fame – in a constructive way and maybe make it heard above that dreadful silence.

Michael: You were a great friend of Rock Hudson and Montgomery Clift before that, was it because of them that you wanted to fight this bigotry?

The one that got away.

That enigmatic smile.

The way we were *after* the fun!

Oh that smile!

Elizabeth: No.

Michael: Just a general cause?

Elizabeth: Yes. Just man's inhumanity to man, and the ignorance and the cruelty and the lack of compassion that people were showing – and still are.

Michael: You're a grandmother of how many children now?

Elizabeth: I have four children, six grandchildren.

Michael: Six. And is it because of them that you're worried about the future – do you get depressed as a grandparent?

Elizabeth: No, I don't – maybe I should. Because it's in our hands, it's in our children's hands and it's in our grandchildren's hands. And I'm an optimist – I think man will save himself before totally dissolving.

Michael: You're an actress; you're a writer; you're a business woman – what's the pattern for the future going to be?

Elizabeth: Keep on going . . .

Michael: I certainly hope you do. Now you have agreed to take questions from our audience here in the studio, on any subject?

Elizabeth: Sure, anything.

Michael: It's wide open, ladies and gentlemen. You, madam, what would you like to ask?

Lady: It is said that men mature as they grow older like a good red wine, but that a woman's beauty fades with age. As one of the world's most beautiful women, how do you feel about this?

Elizabeth: I don't think ageing and beauty really have anything to do with each other. Some of the most beautiful people that I have ever known have been very old, ancient people, because the beauty radiates from within. It's the experience of their lives and their lifetime and what they've done, how they've managed their lives, that shines through and becomes beautiful.

Man: May I ask Miss Taylor if she has any nostalgic

memories of any particular British pubs?

Elizabeth: There is one particular one, I can't remember where it is – I was there years ago. . . .

Man: Could it be in Wood Street, Barnet?

Elizabeth: Well, let me tell you, you'll know which one it is in a second – I went back, obviously years later, and I was having my beer and I finally had to go to the loo and I went into the ladies' room and there was a big sign saying 'Elizabeth Taylor sat here'. Is that the one you mean?

Man: It could well be, yes. I think it might have been The Alexander.

Lady: Miss Taylor, you went to Hollywood as a very young girl and during that time the young actors and actresses such as Mickey Rooney, Judy Garland and Deanna Durbin seemed to be chan- nelled towards song and dance. Were you given a comprehensive study of song and dance? Because I wonder why you haven't made many musicals – you seem to have the personality and the looks for it.

Elizabeth: I did, as a little girl in England, take ballet lessons – all little girls did. I took singing lessons, too, and I actually sang in a couple of films, but if you saw the films you'd see why I'm not in musicals.

Man: Miss Taylor, I think everybody is talking about your appearance but I think you're one of the greatest actresses in the world and I've enjoyed a lot of your films. Last week I saw you in *Suddenly Last Summer* in which I thought you were incredible. What I want to ask you is, in your last film, *Young Toscanini*, you played an opera singer – which opera singer did you base your character on?

Elizabeth: I played a real opera singer from the nineteenth century, Nadena Burokhof and I based myself on her.

Man: And why didn't they just pad you – why did you have to put on weight specially for it?

Elizabeth: I didn't mind really ... I only put on ten pounds – in fact I did look rather skinny amongst all the other opera singers. They're *ample*, it's a lovely word, I think, don't you.

Man: Richard Burton apart, you starred with many leading actors – who has impressed you the most?

Elizabeth: Apart from Richard, Spencer Tracy. I think he started what they now call 'method acting'. I think Spencer Tracy was a sort of originator of *under*playing, *under*stating, *under*acting – he was brilliant.

Michael: Were you very surprised when you yourself won your Oscars?

Elizabeth: I certainly was – especially the first one. I think I got that because of my tracheotomy – I think I probably should have gotten it before, but I'd been a *bad* girl.

Lady: Miss Taylor, can you tell me what your hobbies are? What do you do in your spare time? We thought at one stage we were going to see you motorbiking.

Elizabeth: Well, I have lots of hobbies, collecting things – like diamonds, people – I don't know, I don't really have any specific hobbies. I used to love riding, but I went over a jump seven years ago and the horse stopped, but I kept on going, and I fractured my back, so I thought, I'm too old for that.

Lady: Who had the most influence on your screen career?

Elizabeth: I think I learnt from every director, every actor I've ever worked with. I worked more with Richard than anyone else. And we helped each other and we worked things out together – you know, at home, or when we'd run through the lines. So I think there was more give and take between our performing than any other relationship.

Michael: Research says that Mike Todd was the man who

	awakened you as an actress and as a woman.
Elizabeth:	Where had I been before that?
Lady:	What do you think is the most important aspect of herself a woman should preserve as she grows older?
Elizabeth:	Just keep your sense of awareness, and always be true to yourself.
Lady:	You've obviously enjoyed your career very much and we've all enjoyed you over the years, would you be pleased if your grandchildren went into acting?
Elizabeth:	If that's what they wanted, certainly. One of my sons is an actor and I'm very proud of him. It's not an easy life. One of my daughters is a sculptress, and one was a model but now she's retired and has a baby – whatever makes them happy.
Michael:	Your brother was a beautiful child, wasn't he, but he didn't want to be in the business?
Elizabeth:	No.
Michael:	Was it true that he did something dreadful on the eve of an audition?
Elizabeth:	He was up for a western, and he had the long hair, but after school he went to a barber and had his head shaved. He didn't get the job.
Lady:	Miss Taylor, I've always wanted to ask you – what do you have to think of to make yourself cry in front of the camera?
Elizabeth:	If I started thinking about things ... personal things in my life, I have the feeling I might never stop. So I put my mind at the place where the character I'm playing is, and whatever is making her cry, I work on that and make that affect me. So I become more the other person rather than utilizing and using up my own pain.
Lady:	But how do you actually bring up tears?
Elizabeth:	I don't know. You just squeeze them out.
Michael:	I suppose you could just imagine that ring had slipped off your finger, that would bring a few tears.

Man: Could I ask you a personal question, if it's not too rude – what do you think about when you're lying in the bath?

Elizabeth: It depends on whom I'm dating.

Man: I just always think that that's a moment when you think about – sort of your whole life has gone before you and I just wonder if you....

Elizabeth: No that's when you're drowning.

Lady: Have you ever been approached to appear in *Dynasty* or *Dallas*?

Elizabeth: No.

Lady: And would you appear in them?

Elizabeth: No.

Lady: If you were only allowed one food for the rest of your life, what would it be?

Elizabeth: Vanilla ice cream made from the thickest cream, and hot chocolate fudge.

Man: If you were going to live your life again, how old would you think you'd have to be before you felt mature enough to make the decision to get married?

Elizabeth: I think some people are never mature enough. I don't think you can put an age sort of level on it. I don't think there *is* such a thing as the right age or the wrong age – it depends on the individual. I know I've made a lot of mistakes and there are probably a lot of things I should be sorry about but I wouldn't change my life, I would make the same mistakes because they've taught me so much. The only regrets I have are if I've hurt anyone.

Man: What was it like working with the late John Huston?

Elizabeth: Oh, he was fabulous, he was a wonderful raconteur. He spent most of the time on the phone with his bookie.

Lady: What do you honestly feel about ladies over the age of forty appearing nude in centrefolds such as *Playboy*, and if approached yourself, with the body you have today – which is marvellous –

	would you do it?
Elizabeth:	I *have* been approached and no, I didn't do it and no, I *wouldn't* do it. It's just not my taste.
Lady:	And what do you feel about ladies who do it, such as Joan Collins?
Elizabeth:	If it made Joan happy, fine.
Michael:	They say it made a few other people happy as well . . .
Lady:	You say in your book that many of your problems stem from the fact that you were the wife of an ambitious politician. Do you think that many political wives have the same problems that you had?
Elizabeth:	Yes, I do. I think Washington is the loneliest city in the world for a woman, for that reason.
Michael:	But aren't the wives of politicians chosen to be the perfect wife and therefore fully involved in what he does?
Elizabeth:	There is really no such thing, I think, as a perfect politician's wife, because she has to be so many things, and yet nothing at the same time. Dispensable and totally indispensable. She should be several people.
Michael:	But no real status at all?
Elizabeth:	None. And you never know when your husband is coming home for dinner, or if he's coming home alone, or with his secretary or with a friend – I mean, you have nothing in your life to plan, not even that night, let alone the next day or the weekend.
Man:	Miss Taylor, you must have had a very eventful life – if you could choose to live a part of that life again, which decade would you choose?
Elizabeth:	Oh, I bet you could guess that one.
Michael:	Did it involve *National Velvet* and my asking for an autograph? It took a year for that picture to come, you know.
Elizabeth:	That's because I mailed it myself.
Michael:	I knew you had! I know you don't have regrets because that's not your style. But do you

somehow wish that you had been reunited with Richard Burton?

Elizabeth: I'm sure we will be, some day.

Michael: That was the perfect answer. Your own life has been remarkable for tragedies, and triumphs — it would make a good movie and a good book, are either of those things planned?

Elizabeth: No, I'm too busy living today and looking forward to tomorrow to dwell on the past.

Michael: Well, it's been a joy to meet you this evening, please can I have another signed photo to replace the old one? Thank you very much, Elizabeth Taylor.

After we finished recording, Elizabeth stayed on for a drink, which was a bonus. When we were having a photograph taken after the show, she turned to me and asked, 'Have I got lipstick on my teeth?' I said, 'No, but I wouldn't mind some on mine ...' She just gave a dirty chuckle but later, in the hospitality room, I noticed her glossing up, and then she marched up, got hold of my face and planted a great magenta smacker on my cheek, and held it there for several seconds. I struggled desperately, of course. Lizzie, my wife, took an impression of it on a tissue, so now I have Elizabeth Taylor's kiss in the drawer of my bedside table. What more could I want? Don't answer that.

CHILDSPLAY

The year I was born was an eventful one – Hitler came to power, the Loch Ness Monster was first sighted, and the film *King Kong* was made. Yes, a lot was happening in 1933, but my arrival still managed to create a bit of a stir in the ordinary, working-class South London family that I belonged to. It took me quite a few years to realize that my timing was terrible – the repercussions of being born then were enormous. Old enough to be frightened by the war, but too young to be involved. Even afterwards, when I was a teenager, I paid for my bad timing, coming just too early to enjoy the fun and freedom that waited round the corner.

When I was six years old, my sister Pat eight, and my younger brother Alan three, war broke out. At school they made us try on gas-masks for size, and there was talk of evacuation. Then one day it happened – the three of us were dispatched to Chard, in Somerset, understanding very little of what was happening to us. My sister and brother stayed together, and were sent to a terribly posh house to live with the ex-Mayor of Chard and his two maiden sisters. I went to Rose and Cyril Grabham, a lovely couple who lived at No 4, Park Cottages. At the time I wondered why Pat and Alan stayed together, but I reasoned that Pat, being the eldest, was there to look after Alan, the youngest. I was obviously deemed old enough to look after myself.

Time was impossible to measure down in Chard – it always is when you're a child – and I remember one day chatting to Uncle

Cyril and feeling that I'd been living there for an age. I reckoned it to be about nine months, so I asked him how long it had been. 'Ooh, well, let's see now, I s'pose it must be getting on for six weeks, now,' Cyril said.

But if they were strange times for us, I can hardly imagine what they were like for my mother. One day she had a husband and three children, the next, no one. My father was in the army, we were living in the country, and she stayed and worked in London. The initial shock must have been terrible, but in fact she had rather a good war. She had a lot of fun – somehow, people did.

Four-and-a half years later we were all reunited, back in the tiny flat in Wandsworth. After the wide open spaces of Somerset, everything in London seemed to have shrunk. Pat had returned to London two years earlier, unable to settle with her genteel family in Chard. Alan came home as a Little Lord Fauntleroy, and we had a new baby brother, Geoff. Those years apart did something to us as a family – it was hard to adjust to one another again after so long apart. Alan and I used to fight – but that was just little boys striking out. As adults we had a good relationship, sadly ended by his death in a motorbike accident in 1979.

At school in Somerset, I was a star pupil – keen, confident and bright. The confidence was knocked out of me after I had won a scholarship at the age of eleven and was sent to a school in Hampshire. I was never so self-assured again, though I rallied enough to get some good results in the School Certificate exams, and joined in enough activities – rowing, choir, dramatic society – to be dubbed as an all-rounder by the headmaster (a description which brought jeers from my schoolmates).

The highlights of our childhood were 'Children's Hour' on the wireless, and the cinema. In those days, if you stuck an advert for the cinema in your window, you got free tickets, and long before I ever understood any kind of plot, we'd all troop down to the local flea pit and watch whatever was showing. The wireless and the cinema gave me such enjoyment that I decided I'd become an actor, a film star. But, that was before television came along . . .

Our childhood shapes the kind of people we become, and influences our choice of career, so it's a subject we often turn to on the show. Some of my guests were born sucking on the proverbial silver spoon, others knew hard times. To begin at the beginning. . . .

PATRICK LICHFIELD I had the great advantage of being brought up by a really traditional, old-fashioned nanny, who saw us through numerous disasters, one of which was the very memorable moment during the blitz when we were taken to a very smart tea shop in Curzon Street, a place where nannies met each other and their charges were just kept in tow. My sister and I were sitting there, and the first doodle bug hit the building next door and the entire ceiling started to come down. The waiters ducked under tables and there was a lot of stuff flying everywhere. And this fascinated me because, I mean, the war was very exciting to a child. The next one was a direct hit, and the whole ceiling did come down. And then the dust cleared and there was Nanny, sitting on the other side, and me with my elbows on the table looking at her. I said, 'Nanny, what was that?' And she said, 'That's a bomb, dear. Elbows off the table.'

I spent most of my life travelling from one house to another, from one grandparent or great grandparent to another. It was very nice, I enjoyed it. Some of the houses were haunted, though as a child I didn't know they were haunted. My bedroom, for instance, had a ghost that used to come through it every night – it wasn't a visible ghost but it *was* audible – and I used to see the door open at the other end of the room when I was in bed and then would hear this 'clunk clunk'.... I didn't take much notice of that, and then the door at the other end would open and close. Strangely enough, it didn't occur to me as being odd until I saw my mother frantically spraying the room one day. You know those old Enos bottles? Well, she had some Holy Water in it, and she used to spray it about, and it used to keep them out for a bit, you know.

LES DAWSON We used to live in a house in Manchester in the slums. It was so small if you didn't pay the rent they didn't evict you – they used to flush you out with ferrets.

BILL WYMAN My childhood was very hard. I grew up in Lewisham, South East London, and it was awful because Dad was a bricklayer, and if the weather was bad, he didn't work. He once went two months without working – with five kids. It was quite difficult. If they didn't have food for breakfast for us, they wouldn't wake us up in the morning. They used to let us stay in bed, so it was a bit tough. But it was also great, because we didn't know any different, so we never missed anything.

FRANK CARSON We were so poor we had a chicken in the oven for Christmas, and I opened the door to see how it was doing and the fellow from next door was dipping his bread in the gravy. The nearest thing we got to a jacuzzi was a fart in the bath. Sorry!

ERNIE WISE I was a child prodigy. I was a railway porter's son and I was discovered by a man who had a discovery show just like *Opportunity Knocks*. He took me down to London and I went and did an audition and I first appeared at what is now the Shaftesbury Theatre at the top of Shaftesbury Avenue. I became a star overnight in 1939, and the money was very, very necessary. We were a large family of seven and my father worked on the railway and he only had two pounds a week, but we could make three pounds and ten shillings just at the weekend by working the clubs. I used to have a special gimmick – when I used to do my clog dance, I used to shout to the audience, 'Throw pennies,' and that's what they used to do. And the faster I danced and the longer I went on, the more pennies I got. So I collected them all and took them home. We had enough, we had a roof over our heads and we had enough food and things like that, but nothing for luxuries or little extras.

JULIE CHRISTIE One of my over-riding memories of childhood is being tied to a tree by a nanny. . . . I did wonder if it was a nightmare because it's so vivid . . . have you ever had something you remember from your childhood which was so horrible and awful that you're not quite sure whether it was real or a nightmare? I think it was real, but sometimes I just can't believe anybody did that.

TELLY SAVALAS With the kind of neighbourhood I was from, if you didn't play hookey or steal a lollipop every now and then, you weren't one of the boys. So I came into contact with the police during the course of my growing up, but that, of course, was just a little research for when I did *Kojak*.

BRITT EKLAND My childhood was all about manners and how to hold your knife and fork and which glass to drink out of, and we had to curtsey, and as for my father, well, if I was looking like this – with blonde hair hanging down and the red lipstick – he would say I looked like a slut. He would just make me go and wipe it all off.

DIRK BOGARDE I'm a terribly shy man but I wasn't a shy child. We lived a very open and free life with greatly loving parents who told us everything. We knew where we came from, and why we were born, so there was none of that kind of shyness at all but, I suppose from the ages of twelve, fourteen, fifteen, life suddenly took us over and then I got shy.

My sister and I hated hikers, so we used to get the berries of various poisonous things, and put them in a Kia-ora bottle and shake them all up, leave the label on and screw the lid on, and leave it there with a fake picnic, you know, a few bits of egg shells lying around. This is 1930 I'm talking about, and we hated these new people that came into the country wearing long floppy shorts, and we thought, 'Well, if they take a drink from this bottle, they'll then have diarrhoea in those terrible shorts. Then they'll never, never come back to our village again.' And they never did come back.

KIRK DOUGLAS I was always really, really poor. I tried to explain to my sons what being poor is but it's hard for them to imagine a time when you literally didn't have enough to eat. I do remember one luxury. I was in High School and always wanted to go to the Prom. I never could afford it, but this particular time, I'd saved up all the money. There was a girl I was quite keen on – she was beautiful – and I finally summoned up the courage to ask her if she would go with me to the Prom. She was delighted – and so was I – I had my money saved and I was going to have my nice suit pressed. But the next day I saw her and she seemed to be avoiding me. I didn't know what had happened but finally I caught up with her, and said, 'Mary, is anything wrong?' And tears came into her eyes and she told me that she was sorry but she couldn't go to the Prom with me. I couldn't understand why, and she finally confessed that her father wouldn't let her because I was a poor fellow from the other side of the track, and she lived up on the hill.

FELICITY KENDAL When I was nine months old I was taken out to India by my parents who had a theatre company – they still have it, in fact, and they still tour. But when I was a little tiny baby, we travelled all the time. We went from one corner of the country to another and we stayed in palaces and magnificent hotels and played in beautiful little theatres, and then two weeks later, we'd be in a dark bungalow with cockroaches and snakes in the loo, where they had desks tied together with string for a stage. It was an extraordinary childhood.

JODIE FOSTER I think my childhood was really healthy – I'm sure it wasn't normal and it wasn't like everybody else's but it was a great education. I got to travel all over the place and there was a certain kind of confidence that was instilled into me at a young age. My mum always travelled with me, although there were a few years when I wanted to travel alone. I get very lonely when I work and it's nice having her around because if I'm mean to her, she doesn't hate me for ever, or leave. . . .

BARRY McGUIGAN I was an awful child. I nearly gave my mother a nervous breakdown. I remember when I was about two-and-a-half or three, they used to come in and say to her, 'Mrs McGuigan, we don't want to alarm you but your son is on top of that thirty-foot pole out there,' and my mother would say, 'Oh, that's old hat, let's hear something new.'

DOLLY PARTON I grew up in the great Smokey Mountains of East Tennessee, in a family of twelve children. There were six girls and six boys – Willa, Dean, David, me, Bobby, Stella, Cassie, Randy, Larry, Floyd, Freda and Rachel – in that order. You know, we were happy. We had a lot of hard times but we didn't know we were poor until some smart Alec told us. That was just a way of life back there – we didn't have money but we didn't judge life by money because we were mountain people, country people. We lived on a farm, we raised our own food, we canned our own food, and the only things we ever bought from the grocery store were coffee and sugar. Everything else, we knew how to make, how to grow, how to prepare. It's always a comforting feeling for me – I think, if the worst should happen, at least I'd know how to raise a garden, how to take care of myself and the people close to me.

Before I left home, a lot of my girlfriends' mothers didn't like them to hang around with me because they thought I was a bad influence – just because I wore my clothes real tight, and I wore make-up, and I started bleaching my hair as soon as I could find a way to get some bleach. Mothers would say, 'I don't want you hanging around her,' but I was really as good as good can be. My friends were the ones sleeping in the back seats with the boys, and doing all the things that I just looked like I was doing.

JULIE ANDREWS I guess I was a bit of a show-off. My aunt had a dancing school for many, many years and I appeared in all her plays, and at school I appeared in school plays and I was very proud when I played Robin Hood. I had to slap my thigh and cavort around. I guess I loved to show-off, yeah. But I didn't think I was a pretty child at all. I had a boss-eye and buck-teeth and bandy legs . . . but my mummy loved me.

PETER USTINOV I always wondered why my parents believed all this nonsense about Father Christmas – I was always very sceptical. I remember being terrified of going into Harrods because I thought King Herod lived there, and that I wouldn't come out in one piece. Funnily enough I believed that, but not Santa Claus, but my parents seemed to believe it, so I had to go along with them. I was worrying how to break it to my own children when I was saved. We were in New York, and came round a corner to find fifteen Father Christmases trying to decide whether or not to go on strike. That rather settled the problem.

BERYL REID I had an imaginary friend when I was a child called 'Invigamise-who-was-born' – don't ask me why, because I don't know. My mother used to say to me, 'Beryl you've never been out by yourself again have you?' And I'd say, 'Of course not, Mummy, I know I mustn't do that. Invigamise-who-was-born was with me.'

I was about three then, but I've got a new one now. She's called Ruby Hind. Now she *is* marvellous because whenever I don't want to do a performance on the stage, Ruby will go on for me. She lives behind curtains and things in my dressing-room. But she's no good at the classics. If I'm doing a classical play she can't go on, but she's good with the commoner stuff. Directors know when Ruby is on. They come round at the interval and say, 'Was Ruby on for the first half?' and I say, 'Yes.' They say, 'Well, get her off.'

CHUCK BERRY I've met a lot of prejudice. My father was a carpenter and I went around with him since I was 8 years old, and we worked for a company in the white neighbourhood. The way Dad handled it was to train *me* how to handle it. Dad was very gentle and very subtle about the insults that can come from some of the males in those places. Dad would say: 'I'll have the company send someone else, and thank you.' So by the time I got on the road playing music, and had to go to some of the back windows in the South to get a meal – because there'd be a sign up in the front windows, 'Whites only' – I was ready for it.

TALES OUT OF SCHOOL....

PATRICK MOORE I was ill for a lot of my boyhood, but I did manage one complete term at prep school. I must have been six or seven – something like that – and we had drawing lessons once a week, taken, believe it or not, by a Mr Moore. I was getting some drawing prep once and what I was actually told to draw was a towel hanging over a chair. Only I misheard and thought he said a cow hanging over a chair. So I did – my mother had that drawing for many years – and then Mr Moore rang my mother and said that it was so nice having me in his class because I was so interested and keen, but there wasn't really a lot of point, and wouldn't it be better if I played the piano?

HARRY SECOMBE I remember after an exam in school, the geometry exam, the master picked up my paper and he said, 'We've one boy here who scored a record for the school, no marks at all, nothing, no marks, not even one for neatness.' I later realized that the reason I always did so badly was I just couldn't see the blackboard because I was so short-sighted.

ROY CASTLE I wasn't terribly bright at school. When I was a kid, I was very short-sighted and they didn't have compulsory eye tests at school until I was seven. So until then, I just couldn't see, but, of course, I didn't *realize* that I couldn't see and it was all a blur, because I never knew what it was like to see objects in focus. We used to have a clock and the teacher used to turn its hands round and say, 'Now what time is it?' When it came to me, I didn't know what time it was. I couldn't see the clock – I didn't know they even *had* a clock. But then when I got glasses suddenly the whole world came into focus and I thought, 'So *that's* what it's all about, is it?'

The Hovis ad really is exactly the kind of place that I was born in.

(above) The ten gallon Tony Curtis.

(above right) Pamela Stephenson, the
original headbanger.

(opposite) George Segal, in an early
show, pays tribute to George Formby.

Liza Minelli.

It was one up and one down, terraced on three sides, so you could hear the people poking their fires on three sides. In fact, we didn't have to have our fire on if the other three had theirs on – three hot walls, which was very nice.

My mother made me take up tap dancing, because I'd got sparrow legs. As a kid I was one of those little wiry lads with thin legs, and they all said, 'He's puny, is that lad. You want to send him for dancing lessons.' But it just got me into a lot of fights, that's all. At school, the lads used to say, 'Ha, you're going for your dancing lesson, hee-hee . . . you have to wear a ballet frock.'

JIM DAVIDSON We used to have an old teacher, a great fellow, named Mr Davies who taught us woodwork. He had a limp, he had a false leg, and of course, when you're kids it strikes you as very funny to have a woodwork teacher with a wooden leg, so he'd say, 'What shall we make today, kids?' and we'd go 'Want another leg, sir?' and things like that.

DAVID ESSEX I was confused at school because although I didn't like the way we would dismiss the teachers and what they were trying to teach us, at the same time I wanted to be the ace yob. We had a lovely science teacher called Daddy Dyance. His hobby was breeding bees and one day he brought them in in a glass cabinet and he was saying, 'These are the workers and this is the queen bee, and they fly out of the window and come back with pollen and they make honey.' So my mate Gabby Lawrence thought, 'Well, great.' He got the gas pipe from the Bunsen burner, stuck it in the glass cabinet and gassed the bees. And I'll never forget Mr Dyance. He was saying, 'Now we'll go over to the bees,' and he went over and they were all lying at the bottom. He went nuts – he went crackers, got the cane, and he was wielding it, and it was at that time that the rest of the boys decided to pile up the furniture in the corner and set fire to it, so half the classroom was burning. There's Daddy Dyance diving off desks and whacking boys with the cane – it was that kind of school. They knocked it down later.

TERRY JONES I got one prize at school – for an essay. I spent the whole holiday writing this essay and I won the prize because nobody else entered for it.

PAUL McCARTNEY John Lennon and I used to bunk off school and we'd go to my house, when my dad was out at work. We'd just sit around in the front parlour of my house and smoke Typhoo Tea in my dad's pipe. It was horrible, but we were teenage fools and we wanted to sit at home and do big grown-up things.

CLIFF RICHARD I did quite well at school in the sports area, and for ages and ages I had the school record for the under-14's javelin. . . . And I ran quite well, too. I hated rugby but I always played when they wanted me to because I was really fast. I'd run, and no one caught me, so I never got walloped or anything. I didn't box, although I had a lot of fights at school. When I first moved from India (where I was born) to England, I obviously had a great tan, and I got called 'Indibum' and all that. It's just ridiculous really, but I fought a lot at school. I came home bruised and in tears sometimes, but I gave as good as I got.

We used to listen to a lot of radio, but we didn't have a record player or anything like that for ages. I never had a TV set until I bought one with my first lot of royalties and the only way we got the record player was because my dad won about £40 on the pools. There was a big argument about what we should buy so we had a vote on it. My mum and I voted my dad out and we said we'll have a record player.

TWIGGY We didn't have a record player, but when I was about five, my sister, who's seven years older than me, was a great Paul Anka fan – he was the great love of her life. I remember she went out and bought his record, 'Diana'. But we didn't have a record player, so every night we'd get it out and look at it. It was hysterical . . . I mean, that's really funny, isn't it – we didn't have anything to play it on but we still thought it was great.

NEIL KINNOCK My first ambition was to be a policeman, and then a private detective. I wanted to play for Wales – at anything, tiddly winks, snooker, anything at all. If I could've worn a red jersey that would've been it. I wanted to be a coal miner, and that was a serious ambition, too. My parents went absolutely nuts because all my family are coal miners – my grandfathers, my uncles – and the idea was that if you got a chance you *didn't* go down the pit, but I wanted to. That led to warfare for about three months in our house. Then I wanted to join the army and that was another two months of warfare, and then when I wanted to go in the police force my parents said, 'You're trying to tell us something about your attitude to school, aren't you?' They said, 'Look, go to university and *then* you can do what you like.' I conceded to that and went to university, and of course your whole life changes then.

At school I certainly wasn't a swot, but I wasn't a layabout, either. One of the most flattering things ever said to me was by a teacher who said, 'Kinnock, I'd like to call you lazy but nobody who's as big a nuisance as you are is lazy.' So I wasn't lazy, I was busy at everything all the time, but at all the wrong things. I really didn't have much time for school. What I enjoyed doing most was having a laugh.

LIZA MINNELLI Until I was fifteen I wanted to be an ice skater and I really studied and worked at it – I wanted to be in the Olympics. And then I saw a show called *Bye Bye Birdie* and I thought, 'That looks like more fun!'

There were many good times, in my childhood, but I think people know more about the glum stuff, because that's what writers write about. But my mother had a wonderful sense of humour and so did my father. And I wouldn't have changed any of my childhood. I've met so many people who had much more of a horrendous childhood than I had, but their parents weren't in the public eye. It's just that ours were made very public. I think that's the difference. But then everybody else's parents seemed to be famous, too – I mixed with people like Mia Farrow and Candice Bergen. We all thought it was normal.

GEORGE MICHAEL When I was very young – about 5 years old – I wanted to be a pilot because I had this girlfriend who was going to be a stewardess. And then when I was about seven I went for an eye test where you get one of those cards with all the dots on, and, you're supposed to see fifty-seven but I could only see twenty-seven. And I'm just slightly red/green colour blind. It's not that bad, it's just that red and green are fairly important colours to people who try to wave down planes and things like that, so they told me that being a pilot was definitely out. Luckily, that was about the same time that my mother and father bought me a radio, and all my other interests just disappeared once I had that. . . .

I was one of those people who went through an incredibly

unfortunate period called puberty – basically, my face exploded. Also, as a child I wore very thick glasses and was very overweight ... all the best things that you can possibly be. And I just generally didn't have a clue ... I mean, I was one of those kids who never even saw a mirror until I was about thirteen, and by that time it was too late. So I gave up on the idea of girls until I was about fifteen, when I suppose my hormones calmed down a bit. I was actually very shy, but girls initiated relationships. I was all right from then on. Even today, when I see a bad picture of myself, that thirteen year-old comes flooding back, you know, waddling along.

CLIVE JAMES When I was an adolescent, I was worried because I *didn't* have spots. All the other boys in the class sort of grew up overnight – they all grew a foot taller and their faces were just full of acne. But I didn't have the acne and I didn't grow. So I got envious of them – even of their acne. I was dying of jealousy for guys whose faces were just cratered with seeping yellow pus.

Dances were absolute torture, because I was so small and because my hands sweated a lot. They still do, but I've learnt now to keep them in my lap so that the sweat coming off the hands soaks into the trousers. In those days, the sweat would fall off my hands and I'd hear it hitting the floor. It's very hard to ask the girl you adore to dance if you know your hands are running like taps.

FAMILY MATTERS

A family just keeps you down to earth. It would be very difficult to do my job without one.

– Margaret Thatcher

The great thing about families is that they keep your feet firmly on the ground – sometimes more firmly than you'd like. I've sat at home with relations, preparing to watch the show with them, and they'll sit through the opening music in respectful silence, but as soon as I start to speak, so do they. Or they'll wait until I'm half-way through a sentence, and get up to go to the loo. One evening when we were watching the show, I looked around and discovered I was the only person awake in the room. Even the dog was asleep, and that was in the first five minutes. I suppose that's the good thing about families – nobody pretends. Of course there's no one more supportive when the chips are down, and no one is prouder of you when you've done well than your old mum . . .

JULIE WALTERS I used to do impressions and my granny, I suppose, was the first. She was Irish, a wonderful woman. She survived two strokes, and my brother and I used to say 'At the third stroke' – We did, it was a great joke – he was only twelve, my brother.

When I first decided to go into acting, my mother went mad – it was quite understandable, we didn't know anything about the acting profession. And she went bananas when I said I was going to leave nursing, which is a really respectable profession and stable and all that kind of thing. But now it's 'My daughter the actress – have you seen her latest film?' I've only made one, but never mind. . . .

OMAR SHARIF My mother is still a very strong influence on me. She decided when I was born, that I was going to be somebody very famous although she didn't quite know for what. And consequently she brought me up that way. When I was learning to write, we had to write between two lines, and if my 'a' or my 'b' went a little bit over the line I used to get a hiding. She used to lay me on the bed, take her slipper off and give me a good beating. And I had one every day – she always had something to beat me for, because what she expected of me was perfection, which of course is impossible. And I think it made me very competitive. My mother still buys my clothes, she does everything. She's very proud of me. She goes into stores and she says to all the people there. 'I'm Omar Sharif's mother,' and she is surprised if they don't rush around and help her with what she wants. She sees everything with the eyes of love. I mean, the worst films I've made – and there are a lot of them – she loves, she thinks I was terrific. It was she who started me gambling. When I was a young lad, I never remember seeing my mother when she *wasn't* sitting at a gambling table. Our apartment was like a casino, she was always gambling. I got up and went out to school and she was dealing. I got back and there she was, the same game, with the same people – playing poker. She had to sell all her jewels, and she lost all her money gambling.

BERYL REID My mother was absolutely marvellous about me going on the stage. She was a Scots Presbyterian from Edinburgh and knew nothing about the theatre, but just knew I was going to do it. And that was it. I went for an audition for a pantomime and she said, 'Now don't forget, Beryl, there's nothing you can't do.' And so I went to see Jack Gillam and he said, 'What do you do?' I said, 'Everything.' I was terrible, mind you. No good at all. He said, 'How much money do you want?' and I said, 'Three pounds a week.' And he said, 'Do you know, all my life I've been looking for somebody who could do everything for three pounds a week.'

FRANKIE HOWERD My mother was a very quiet lady but she used to enjoy being at my parties and what she used to enjoy most of all, oddly enough, was doing the washing up. She was not one for showing off, she just liked to do the washing up and be there and look after everybody. I remember Richard Burton was very fond of my mother.

DUSTIN HOFFMAN My mother was dying during the time we were working on *Tootsie*. She'd been a very vital woman and suddenly, at the age of 73, she had a heart attack. She had this great little body – she was 4 feet 11 inches – and she still played tennis. She and my dad lived about forty miles away and I used to visit a great deal when we were working on the script of *Tootsie*. I'd talk to her about the script and she loved it. She kept saying, 'This is the best role you've had, this is the one.' And I found that I put a lot of my mother's characteristics into Dorothy Michaelson. Sadly she didn't live to see it, but she's in the movie. There's a photograph of her there. It was funny because we were making a comedy yet this character was always making me sad.

ANNEKA RICE I think my mother worried about those hair-raising moments in *Treasure Hunt*. She often rang up the producer and had a go at him and made him swear never to do anything like that again.

LAUREN BACALL My grandmother would have disapproved of Bogie for religious reasons. My mother disapproved of him because she was his contemporary, and she thought, 'This man's been married three times, why *wouldn't* he love a beautiful nineteen year-old girl?' She was very suspicious of him and you can hardly blame her. But she came around and they adored one another. They became really good friends because they were very alike.

MEL BROOKS When I told my mother I was going to marry a Catholic, we couldn't hear her answer – her head was in the oven . . .

MAUREEN LIPMAN When I took Jack [Rosenthal] home for the first time it was my parents' silver wedding anniversary. We had a photograph taken of all the family and my mother kept saying, 'Could you move a little further over there, Jack, move a bit more . . .' By the end of it he was standing on his own, and I said to my mother, 'Why did you do that?' She said, 'In case nothing came of it, I could cut him off.'

TWIGGY My mother won't travel. I mean, she'll go on a bus but no further, and we tried everything to get her to come to America – she would have loved to see me on Broadway, and she wanted to get there. If we could have beamed her down like in *Star Trek*, it would have been all right, but she just couldn't cope with getting on a plane or a boat.

DAD'S ARMY

CHARLOTTE RAMPLING Mine was a military family. My father was a Colonel and we wandered around England and ended up in France, which is the reason I speak French. I live in France now, and I'm married to a Frenchman, but my introduction to drama was through an amateur dramatic society in Stanmore, where we were living at one time. Each year they asked all the people to do little sketches, and as my sister and I spoke French, we thought it might be quite fun to do a kind of singing and dancing cabaret act – it was quite risqué at the time – I was fourteen – and in fact we were spotted by a talent scout who wanted us to come up and audition for a show in a London night club. All went fine, and we were very chuffed and thrilled, until the producer of the show started to say, 'Well, of course, you acted with belted raincoats and the berets and it's all very sweet, but maybe we could start to take off the belted raincoat, and leave perhaps just the fishnet tights ...' Well, you can imagine the Colonel at that stage said emphatically 'NO', and so my debut into cabaret was dramatically finished.

HELEN MIRREN My father was born in Russia and his father was a colonel in the Tsarist army. He was sent over to make an arms deal with the British government and being a military man he was extremely loyal and a little blinkered. He really didn't think the Revolution was anything more than a few peasants kicking up a fuss, like they had been doing for hundreds of years. So he brought his family over because negotiations were taking so long, and he basically got cut off. So he went from being an immensely rich aristocrat in Russia to being a taxi driver – all in about four years.

My parents would go and stand outside the Aldwych theatre just to see the audience going in to see me. They'd just watch, thinking, 'Oh, they're going to see my daughter.' It was very touching.

ROBERT KILROY SILK My father was killed during the war, and my mother married his best friend. This man and my father had joined up on the same day, they went to the same school, played football together, both courted my mother and both fell in love with her – and she ended up marrying them both. My name was Robert Silk, and his name was Kilroy. He brought me up as his own son, and was very proud of me as his son. But he refused to adopt me, and refused to change my name, because he said, 'No, he's Billy's lad ... I'll bring him up as my own but he's keeping his own father's name.' So I had two families then, the Kilroys, and the Silks. It was my headmaster who suggested I used both names and so that's what I did.

DAVID JASON My father was a porter at Billingsgate. He was a bit of a character – he'd have to get up at about four o'clock in the morning to cycle to work, and during the war, he was hurtling along during a blackout when suddenly the road disappeared and he went careering into a bomb crater, about 50 feet wide and 40 feet deep. When he came to about twenty minutes later he couldn't get out. He started shouting for help and about ten or fifteen minutes later, two chaps arrived and a couple of torches shone down on my father at the bottom. 'Go on,' said my dad, 'get me out of here, will you, lads?' And one of these old chaps said, 'Bloody hell, he's had a 50-ton bomb dropped on him and the bugger's still alive!'

TELLY SAVALAS My father was a millionaire three times over and a pauper four. He was the kind of guy who never said no to anything. He arrived in America, and didn't know any languages. You know what his first job was? He was an interpreter.

ANJELICA HUSTON My father would often go to Africa and return with parrots on his hand, then he'd go to Rome and return in black leather suits. I think he and Tom Jones were the only people in those days who actually dressed that way. On the last film he made, although he was very frail, he was mentally stronger than anyone around – it was sort of embarrassing to be walking around on your feet because it seemed that everyone else should be in a wheelchair with tubes in their noses. He was frail physically, but so strong and astute mentally. It was inconceivable that he would die. It was sheer will that kept him going – that and movies.

NIGEL HAVERS Just imagine being a kid and having such a legal background. If ever I told a little lie, my father [Sir Michael Havers, former Attorney General] could tell just like that. And I was always cross-examined over the breakfast table. Then later, when I was at drama school, my father had a flat in the Temple which is where all these lawyer chaps hang out. And I used to use this flat because although I had to pay Dad a bit of rent, of course, it was quite low. People would come and stay the night and then they'd be there a month, you know how it is: 'Can I stay a night?' 'Sure, sure.' Three months later and they're still there. I remember one occasion when Dad turned up on a Sunday – a bit unfair, I thought – and there were fourteen people staying and twenty shirts quietly soaking in the bath. He just said, 'I want this place cleaned up in forty minutes.'

JOHN HURT My father is a practising Minister, living in Scotland. I think my parents got used to my outrageousness from an early age. I really enjoyed getting people going – yes, I'm well acquainted with the wooden spoon.

LORETTA SWIT My dad was my greatest fan. . . . I just finished six months in a play and he was there every matinee, whenever he could get into the city, just sitting in the audience, smiling and beaming and just loving it – 'That's my little girl.'

RUBY WAX My father's very proud of me. When I joined the Royal Shakespeare Company, I did it for him. One night, after the show, we had a big dinner, and there was Michael Hordern and Jane Lapotaire, and Ian Charleson, and my father says, 'I'll pay, I'll pay, you're Ruby's little friends.' And they're saying, 'No, Mr Wax, you don't have to do that.' And then he said what he always says – 'Listen, when you're famous, you can pay for me!'

I have to call my family about twice a week just to check that the inheritance is still cooking over. 'How's the stocks coming?' I say, then I hang up.

GEORGE MICHAEL I spent my whole childhood – from the age of about seven until the day I got my record contract – having rows with my parents ... specifically my father, because he's not very musical, to put it mildly. I can't blame him. I mean, he had no idea about what possibilities there were for me and he just looked at it as a very, very dodgy profession to want to go into. Now of course he sits at home and waits for the cheques! He's great, he came round very soon with a lot of dignity – he just accepted that he'd been wrong.

About two or three years before WHAM! started, Andrew Ridgley was already wearing two earrings. And my mum and dad didn't like Andrew very much. My dad said to me, 'You ever come home with two earrings and you'll be out that door, right?' My dad's Cypriot and I think he meant what he said. And then the day after we got our record contract, I went to Selfridges and had both my ears pierced. And I went home, through the door in absolute fear ... and not a word was said.

Now my mum and dad come to just about every concert. My mother's amazing – she's so reserved, and very English, yet the minute the curtain goes up, she's down at the front. Half way through a number I've seen a commotion going on and it's Mum, trying to climb the barriers.

KIRK DOUGLAS My father really should've been an actor. He was a very physical, violent man, very powerful and he was not around the house much. I remember one critical period in my life, we were all sitting around the table, my six sisters and myself, and we never said a word and we were all drinking tea, Russian-style, in a glass. And my father was breaking off a piece of sugar and sipping the tea through the sugar and something told me that if I don't do this thing I had in mind, I would die. My sisters looked at me in horror as I took a spoonful of hot tea and I flicked it right in my father's face. He jumped up, he grabbed me, picked me up, and he threw me through a door on to a bed. As I look back at it, I remember the feeling of *having* to do it. I thought, I'm going to be killed, but I felt I had to take that risk and I really feel that that was a very important moment in my life.

BARRY McGUIGAN My grandfather had a very bad temper. I used to work with him in my mother's shop – he worked there for twenty-five years, until he died a few years ago. I used to weigh spuds and fill the shelves and all that sort of thing. And I remember one time he gave me a list of things to do in the morning – fill this with potatoes, put the beans up on the shelves, brush the yard and then you can go out. So, it was a Saturday morning and my brother said, 'Come on; lets have a game of football.' I said, 'No, Pappa said do this.' So my brother said, 'Don't worry about Pappa.' So off we went out and we played our football, and I came back, and we were sneaking in through the back door and bumped right into him. So he went at me, but I ducked and he hit the shelf – he broke his thumb in two places! After that he always used to say to me, 'Don't get me mad, now.'

PATRICK LICHFIELD I had enormous parental opposition to being a photographer. The army was all right, but then I should have gone into agricultural life. I could have been a cricketer – I had two uncles who captained the English counties years ago – but a photographer, no. In the '60s that was just considered the worst.

SIBLING HARMONY

KIRK DOUGLAS I was the only boy – I had six sisters, and their affection was almost overwhelming. I've always been indebted because my sisters permitted me to go to college and get an education. I should have stayed home like they did, helping to work and to support the family.

GEORGE MICHAEL I had the good fortune to have two older sisters around the house, who basically had to do all the nasty dirty work. I was one of the typical Greek boys who were allowed to do exactly what they liked and nobody questioned it. It's taken me about a year to realize that the things I put down don't actually disappear of their own accord. And that if you don't pick them up and put them back where you got them from, they are still there two weeks later, and the house looks a bit of a tip. And so now I'm just starting to become vaguely house proud.

CLIFF RICHARD I've got three sisters, and did they spoil me rotten! I think it was fortunate that I was the eldest. I think if you're going to be the only boy, you've got to be the eldest. I kind of ruled the roost a bit, but we got on well.

My dad always brought me up saying you never lay a finger on a woman, never ever. My sister – the one just younger than me – and I used to share all the jobs in the house – if she washed up one day I did the drying up and so on, but when my grandad came to live with us, he thought the world of her so he did all her jobs, and she'd come to me and taunt me, and that used to incense me. So one day, I got a newspaper, I rolled it up and I walloped her like mad. And when my father came home he said, 'Your sister's crying, have you touched her?' I said, 'Never touched her, never laid a finger on her. I have to confess that I walloped her with a newspaper but I didn't touch her.'

DENNIS TAYLOR Alex Higgins once took a fancy to my sister Milly and I wasn't too pleased. He came to our house and knocked on the door and asked if he could use the toilet, because it was a good way of getting in. But my mother knew who it was, so she quickly hid Molly underneath the stairs and that was that, otherwise we might have been brothers-in-law.

TELLY SAVALAS I've got the hairiest brothers you ever saw in your life. . . .

TRACEY ULLMAN Now that I'm famous, whenever I speak to my family, all they want is a signed photo for Enid or Ethel or someone at the office. But they keep my feet on the ground – they don't treat me any differently.

GETTING STARTED

I was a plasterer. I'm an electrician as well. Do you know, I actually did a job in Belfast and I put a spade through a six-inch trunk cable and blacked out Northern Ireland. They're still looking for me.

— Frank Carson

I began broadcasting when I was twenty-one — it was what I wanted to do more than anything, if you don't count an early ambition to be Hopalong Cassidy or Flash Gordon — and I don't think I've had many happier moments than acting in my first radio play. I felt then that at last the ambitions I'd had for so long were possible, and that I could stop worrying about the gypsy who'd looked at me closely a couple of years earlier, and said: 'You'll never come to anything, you won't.' For a while it seemed that she might be right. I left school at sixteen — a job in a publishing company came through the school employment system and that was it. I've often wished that I had stayed on and tried for university, but I wasn't keen, and my family wasn't the sort to encourage it. 'Not for the likes of us,' was the philosophy. These days we're more like the Americans — anyone can do anything and all that nonsense about where you come from and how you speak doesn't matter. But undeterred by background or family opinion, I'd written to the BBC to let them know of my ambitions to be a broadcaster — and was dismissed without benefit of an interview. Nothing put me off, I'm happy to say, but in the years before I got the chance to enjoy what I did for a living, I still had to pay the rent. So after completing my National Service, I did all the things that everybody does when they're trying to break into show business, urged on by my father's insistence that I found employment of some sort – 'Get a job, any job, just get one!' After all, I'd been out of the Army a full six weeks by then. I became a shop assistant, a gardener's labourer, a furniture porter, a salesman – the list went on.

Eventually, in 1954, I went for an audition to the BBC in Cardiff. I arrived at the studios laden with books containing pieces to read. I've always had an ear for accents, and I gave them my best German and Italian and my speciality: French with a hint of Punjabi. Just as I was leaving the studio, I was summoned back. 'Mr – er – Aspel, could you do an Irish accent?' Yes I could, and that's what landed me my first part – Captain O'Hagarty, a dastardly villain in a 'Children's Hour' serial. I had to take time off work, which didn't go down too well with the furniture store which employed me, and I was promptly given the sack. It didn't matter – I was on the way.

Many of my guests have followed similarly tortuous paths before finding their true metier. Some of them could be useful to know. . . .

DAVID JASON I was an electrician before I went into acting – I did all the wiring in my house. Anything you want, just let me know and I'll give you a good price.

GARY WILMOT My first job was as a carpenter. I started a five-year apprenticeship – and lasted three months. I had to finish because I started trying to make everybody laugh. And by the end of about a month, the guy I was assigned to work with refused to work with me because I was always cracking jokes – he said 'I'm not going to work with you, if you crack one more joke I'm going to the supervisor.' And I said 'All right then' and I cracked a joke and he did go to the supervisor. But one of the happiest jobs I ever had was working in a place called Lonsdale Sports. I was a messenger and then I got a job as a shop assistant, later, funnily enough, to be filled by Frank Bruno. Can you imagine Frank as a shop assistant? 'You gonna buy or not, Harry? You did say keep the change, didn't you?' At school they encourage you to get yourself a trade – 'Get yourself a trade and you can't go wrong,' they say. And of course show business isn't considered a trade or a craft, but it really is. I was 22 or 23 before I decided to tread the boards.

JOANNA LUMLEY I worked in a shop which sold very beautiful furniture and rather up-market Swedish glass. I was only there for

The night that Oliver Reed *nearly* joined Su Pollard, Clive James and myself.

Dame Edna strikes again! Lauren Bacall loves it — even Richard Gere is amused.

One of those interesting combinations: John Cleese, Yoko Ono
and Boy George.

'Small fee, small hit.' The inimitable Chuck Berry.

about three months and then I went to a modelling school. You had to go to a modelling school where you learnt how to get in and out of cars with your legs just so, so that nobody could see your knickers. And you learnt how to say, 'Thank you' and wear blue eye make-up. It wasn't really a great help. I became a house model for the great designer Jean Muir and it was a wonderful foundation because she was meticulous. You had to stand and have the clothes made on you, and just when I thought they looked wonderful, she'd go RIP! and snatch a whole sleeve off. Then you had to show the clothes when the buyers came in – people from America or from the grand shops. Sometimes you had to get sandwiches for other people's lunch and run errands, deliver clothes. Once I remember having to work the switchboard when one of the girls was away on holiday – awful – I kept cutting people off. Rows of little switches and lights: beep! 'Yes, hello? One moment, I'll put you through,' click!

CHARLTON HESTON When I first got married and times were lean I was a model for art students doing life drawing. The men got to wear little jockstraps. My wife was doing very well as an actress by that time, but I had not yet begun. She made me a little grey velour jockstrap. I wish I had saved it, I would have brought it along.

GRIFF RHYS JONES I was a bodyguard for a little while – not a very successful one, really, I was the weediest bodyguard that you've ever seen, but I was hired to look after the Sheikh of Quatar – she's a female. We just sat (there were two of us) one on either side, outside her door at the end of a long corridor in The Inn On The Park hotel. I think the principle was that if the terrorists came round the corner, then they'd make such a noise shooting us that they'd wake up everybody inside and give them time to lock the door, and that was really our only role. I did it for about six months here and there. Extremely boring job, we just sat there, and did nothing. Later on, we were on another job, looking after a defence minister from somewhere or other. We'd heard he had thirty billion pounds to spend on tanks and things and we reckoned that when he left he'd probably have a little bit left over for a tip. We finished our shift at 8 and he was going at 9, but at 8, instead of the usual people who came to take over from us, the managing director of the company and his next-door neighbour came in their golfing clothes to pick up whatever tip was being given and we were told to push off. Well, we weren't having that, so we stood around, we said 'Well, we thought we'd just wait around a little bit, you know, just in case they might want to say goodbye to us.' And at that moment, the two people that *usually* took over from us came round the corner, poked their heads round and said 'Oh hello, fancy seeing you here, we just thought we'd pop round to say goodbye.' We were all having a furious argument about who should be there to land this enormous tip and while we were doing that, his Royal Highness sort of sneaked out and didn't give anything to any of us.

JIMMY TARBUCK I used to be a hairdresser. I was awful, I was really, really bad, but I just loved it, life was great fun in those days. One day an elderly lady with a hearing aid came in and I was doing her hair, chatting away and making her laugh, and I cut right through the wire! But she was still smiling at me, so I just tied it in a knot and left it.

I worked at Butlin's in the kitchens first. I was a chargehand and then I just drifted into being a Redcoat, and getting up and doing five minutes on stage and enjoying it. They were great days. It was like *Hi De Hi* backstage, very much so.

OLIVER REED I was a mini cab driver once – when it was very unpopular. We'd drop old ladies off at Victoria Station and the black cab drivers used to be very grumpy with us – in fact they used to punch you very hard in the mouth. So when I used to drop the old ladies off, I'd always give them a kiss goodbye – then the other drivers would think they were my granny!

JAN FRANCIS I was with the Royal Ballet company for four years professionally. It was very, very hard work. I've always said it's like being a race horse, you have to train so hard. I don't think I'm really a naturally disciplined person, but now I can't help it. I'm never late for things, I try really hard to be late, but I just can't be because we were told off so much about it. My poor old feet did suffer and I had to have them sorted out not so long ago. They were absolutely horrid and if I went on the beach, the first thing I did was to dig a hole in the sand to put the feet in and then just stay there all day.... Then I injured my knee, and during the time I had off to get my knee better, I discovered that there was life outside the ballet. I went to the theatre, and met people – you know, I never met many people. And after that I couldn't really get back into it. I just didn't have the enthusiasm.

CLIVE JAMES I had many, many jobs. I was a bus conductor for twelve days – eleven days of training and one day as a bus conductor. Because when the bus came through Pitt Street in the rush hour – Pitt Street was the main street of Sydney – everyone was fighting to get on. It was 100°F outside the bus and 140°F inside, and the bus was so jammed I couldn't move. My job was to press the button to tell the driver to start the bus and then the automatic doors puffed closed and the bus moved off. I only found out later that the back doors had puffed closed over the neck of an old lady who was trying to get on and her head, with a black hat with waxed fruit on it, was inside the bus, and the rest of her, carrying two full shopping bags was outside, running sideways. Luckily, the bus wasn't going as quickly as it would have had there been no traffic, but it was still doing twenty-odd mph. I finally realized something was up because people were yelling at me – I thought they were just trying to get on but then I realized what was up, and I hit the button again. The bus crashed to a halt, the doors puffed open and she dropped to the road. And then she apologized for causing me trouble!

ANNE DIAMOND Many years ago I was a teacher but I was no good at that at all. I taught at a private primary school for girls and really, compared with what some teachers go through, I had a terribly easy time, but I still couldn't cope. There was one little girl there called Isobel, who must be twenty-something now, but she was about nine then, and a right handful. In the middle of a French lesson I was taking, she stood on her desk and started to do a strip. And of course all the other little girls were singing 'The Stripper' - di da da da, di da, da da – and she was doing the full works. I just didn't know how to cope so I sent her out of the room. But by then various other children were misbehaving too, so I sent them out, and suddenly I realized that half of my class was outside the door having a whale of a time!

DAVID ESSEX I started off as a drummer. It was strange really because I didn't know what I wanted to do. It was either small-time crookery or the docks, and I thought, well, the crookery's better, really. I used to go on these escapades with a mate of mine who's now a milkman, and we'd go to Soho, and I remember walking along Wardour Street and hearing this music coming out the basement. I went downstairs, I was just so struck by musicians and live music. I was about fourteen and, I just knew I had to be a musician. The next decision was to find an instrument that I could learn quickly. Bang a drum and it answers back, so I was working on a street market at the time and I went and bought a drum and started to learn.

NIGEL HAVERS My brother, myself and two friends, had a bit of a pop group. We were unbelievably bad but amazingly, we made a record. We called ourselves January – so inspiring – and we made this record which sold 3000 copies. There used to be a programme that introduced new records on the radio, and my father was sailing somewhere and he had this little transistor all primed up, and he said proudly to his friend, 'This is my sons' record' and at that moment a wave hit the boat and the radio went overboard. He never heard it. I think that record was doomed from the start.

I was never cut out to follow family tradition and stick to law – my brother did that for me, bless him. He did all the right things and so I had a way out. I always wanted to be an actor since I was about five and my parents would take me to the cinema and theatre. It seemed to me a natural thing to do. I was just surprised that not everyone wanted to be an actor.

I've now been in this game for about eighteen years and I suppose thirteen of them I didn't have two beans to rub together. I used to do all sorts of other jobs to keep going – I used to be so confident that work was round the corner that when I became a cellarman in a wine shop, I said to my family, 'Of course, I'll only be here for a week or two, you know,' and a year later I was still there. I became the manager of one shop, I was there so long. Then I worked for Jimmy Young for quite a long time ... he saved my bacon. I worked as a researcher for him for so long I became part of the furniture, I really did.

OVERTURE AND BEGINNERS....

FRANKIE HOWERD I trod the boards, as it were, when I was thirteen. I was a Sunday School teacher – don't you see my halo glowing? – and I was in the church Dramatic Society. I used to stutter a lot in those days, I was a very frightened boy. But they were very kind and they gave me a part in this play, it was called *Tilly of Bloomsbury*. And I played Tilly's father with a beard on. We got a few laughs and the local press gave me a good write-up, and the church warden came to me and he said to me 'Frank, you should be an actor,' and I thought God had spoken because in those days, he *was* representing God as far as I was concerned. . . . So I went in for a scholarship with the Royal Academy of Dramatic Arts. There was the board of governors sitting at the back on this cold grey Monday and I got up and I did some Shakespeare and by the time I finished, dawn was breaking. So I went home, and it was just like *Wuthering Heights* where I lived. I went into this field and I sat there and cried for hours in this pouring rain and I suddenly thought to myself, 'This is ridiculous, this is no good – you're not meant to be an actor, you're meant to be something else – a comedian.' And that was it.

MARGARET THATCHER I can remember the moment I decided I wanted to be a politician really quite well. I was at university and it was in recess and we were having a social evening in a village hall and I was staying with a friend. And we went back late and just talked and talked. She had quite a large party staying in the village and so we just gathered in the kitchen and talked. And I was asked about my interests, and naturally I began to talk about politics. But I had never really formed any ambition to become a Member of Parliament, I just talked about things which I love to talk about till all of a sudden one of the guests said: 'You want to be a Member of Parliament don't you?' and I said, 'Yes'. Someone else had to crystallize the feeling, but then I knew it was what I wanted to be. 'Did I think, then, there could be a woman Prime Minister?' I think I was asked at one stage, and I said 'No, not in my lifetime.' But you can't foresee what's going to happen, no one can.

LENNY HENRY It all began when I won *New Faces*, but it gave me a very big head. Girls, money, fast cars – it was the choice between that and working in a factory for the rest of your life, and I went for the girls – 'I'll have the girls and all the money, please.' It was a case of, 'I'll do anything, what do you want me to do? Show biz? Fine.'

ERNIE WISE Originally, I met Eric [Morecambe] in Swansea of all places. I was taller than him in those days, would you believe. And we stayed in digs together once in Oxford, and later I didn't have anywhere to stay and his mother put me up. And from then on we did the double act. The whole 45-year partnership was based on a handshake – no written contract at all. You don't need contracts in this world, not if you trust people and you have an understanding – and let's face it, we needed the money, we stuck together.

JACKIE COLLINS I first started to write at school and I'd charge a few pence for each story – you should have seen what I was writing for the girls. I soon realized that if I made it a bit spicy, I'd get more than threepence for it, so I used to make up limericks, things like,

> 'T'was on the good ship *Venus*,
> My God, you should've seen us . . .'

No, I can't go on any further!

VICTORIA WOOD When I was at school I was hopeless, hopeless. I was the one with the insulating tape round the glasses and a face like Dick Whittington's hankie. I couldn't do anything. We used to do needlework and we had to make a needlework apron in gingham, with lots of pockets for your buttons, and your thread, and your bottle of gin and all that. . . . And it took me longer to do that than it took me to do tapestry. It was like an old dishcloth by the time I was finished. I couldn't do anything, I was hopeless. But I did write one thing at school, the school pantomime, which nobody wanted to be in anyway. Later, at University, I used to do reviews and things like that. I used to try and act in straight plays but I was so bad they made me act with my back to the audience. They said, 'Well, nobody will notice her if she's got her back to the audience,' but all the audience wanted to know was 'Why has that girl got her back to the audience, is she hideously scarred?'

But the reason I started performing was because of my boyfriend at the time – he writes *Coronation Street* now so he's doing all right, no sympathy. We used to write songs together and then one day he wanted to get rid of me. . . . I remember, it was when flared trousers had just come in – remember when you had straight trousers and you wanted to make them into flares you sewed in a triangle of material? Well, I was doing this for him in a loving sort of wifely way and he said, 'Oh, by the way, I want to get rid of you' and I said, 'Thank you very much' and he said, 'Well, finish the trousers and post them on.' So I did – I can't believe it – I wouldn't do it now. But then I thought, 'I'll show him,' and I went in for the Pub Entertainer of the Year contest. God knows why, because I wasn't entertaining and I never went in pubs, but it seemed a good idea at the time. I went in for it and I came third. There was a woman in hot-pants who won, I can't think why, and a man came second who was dressed as a skeleton who climbed out of a coffin and sang. I came third. But I didn't give up, I went in for another and I came third again, and *then* I gave up, so that was the end of that. Then I did get a break because I was at a party where there were lots of television producers who like to relax and let their hair down, fall out of windows and things like that. And they were all relaxing and I was playing the piano and people were all gathered round saying, 'You hit it with the poker, and I'll lock the lid' - but somebody came on and said 'This girl is marvellous, give her a job.' And they did, because they were all drunk as well, and that's how I got where I am today.

JILL GASCOINE I was in the Esther Williams Aqua Show at Wembley in 1956. I was one of her daisies and it meant that we had all these hats on, which were very unattractive – a rubber hat and on top was the daisy, so when you swam around and the people looked down at you, they just saw these daisies. We had on these green woollen leotards which got very heavy when they got wet. And we had to hoist ourselves up out of the water and then go and dance – it was dreadful.

MICHAEL CAINE My mother was prepared to back me in anything I wanted to do. Mainly to get me out of the house, probably, but when I told my father I was going to be an actor he immediately thought I'd turned gay. Except, of course, that gay used to be a word where people were having a happy time. Back then it was called 'nancy boys' which was what my father used to call homosexuals, and he thought that all actors were homosexuals, so I couldn't tell him that everyone in the company that I first joined *was* homosexual – except me. I remember going on tour with an all-male cast and every time we got to any town we used to run and get the paper to see if some show with a chorus was on, because we knew all the guys were gay and all the girls were free.

FELICITY KENDAL I arrived from nowhere, I hadn't been to drama school. I'd been to thirteen convents but I hadn't really been to school properly because I was working by the time I was thirteen. I stayed with my mother's parents in Eltham and I wrote to every theatre company and virtually every person in the world, but nobody would even look at me because I hadn't done drama school. Then a film that I'd made in India opened, and the producer of the film gave me a list of agents' names, and said, 'You are going to be a star. This is the list of all the people you have to ring up.' One of these unlikely people was Malcolm Muggeridge. How I thought he could help me I don't know, but he invited me for lunch, anyway, and he was lovely. I got a job eventually, but it took a long time.

SIGOURNEY WEAVER My father, who was President of NBC, gave me a list of names and I started with the first one, whom I sort of knew. I called him and said, 'I'm just out of drama school and I wonder if I can come in and meet some casting people.' However, he said, 'Do yourself a favour, kid, get a job at Bloomingdales,' which is like your Harrods, and I never called another friend of my father's – I couldn't take the discouragement.

HARRISON FORD I was called in to the Vice President of Columbia Pictures, and he said, 'Kid, I want to tell you a story' – he always called me kid, that always made me feel very small – he said, 'Kid, the first time Tony Curtis ever was in a movie he delivered a bag of groceries. And you took one look at that guy and you knew that that was a movie star.' And I was young and foolish so I said, 'I thought you were supposed to think that that was a grocery delivery boy.' It resulted in him throwing me out.

DUDLEY MOORE My first public performance was behind a chair – I refused to sing unless I had a chair in front of me. I don't know why, I think it was that familiar feeling of being behind bars. I wanted to be a violinist – that was my real ambition – but I was too anxious to really get to grips with the instrument. In fact when I was about twelve, I wrote a piece of music called 'Anxiety' – it was so silly that I framed it.

CLINT EASTWOOD I was doing this film and Rock Hudson was the lead. He was the big wheel there at that time, it was about my second or third film, a bit part, I was playing a lab technician. Then the guy at the studio says 'By the way, I think you should wear glasses because you'll look much more astute, like you're a technician.' I didn't want to wear glasses, and I was thinking how I could get out of it but finally they brought in a bunch of pairs of glasses and I was trying them on in the mirror, and I tried on a pair and I thought, 'Gee, these don't look too bad'. In fact, I came to the conclusion that I looked rather good in glasses. And then we started the rehearsal scene and Rock Hudson walks in and he took one look at me and says, 'Where are my glasses?' He said, 'I'm the physician here, I think I should wear glasses.' So he went through all the glasses until finally they said to me, 'Take yours off,' and they fitted Rock Hudson perfectly, and he looked in the mirror and said, 'I think I look rather good in glasses.'

KATE O'MARA My first ambition was to be a concert pianist, but I come from a long line of actors and I suppose it was inevitable really that I'd follow them. I'm the fifth generation of a family that has been involved in the theatre ... they've built theatres, run companies, been actors, married actresses. And my mother was always making me and my sister perform regularly. We always had to get up little plays and things and do concerts that were absolutely ghastly, but it was a good way of introducing one to it, I suppose.

STEVE DAVIS I fell in love with snooker when I was about fourteen, but when I got to about sixteen or seventeen, I started travelling around and playing in junior competitions and realized that I was very good. Having not gone outside my own area until that point I hadn't realized how good I was. I remember my first-ever game, it was at a place called The Golden Sands Holiday Camp, and they had one snooker table, right next to the miniature railway – it used to be very off-putting when you were playing in the holiday camp competition. I got beaten in the first round but my father was very good – he won the tournament and won a vacuum flask.

LULU A lot of people say, 'Oh how fantastic to have started in the Sixties.' And it *was* but there was a lot of madness and I was pretty frightened by a lot of things that were going on. There were a lot of mad parties – I'd be invited to quite a few of them, and people were walking around a lot of the time saying: 'Hey man, I'm an orange . . .' And I'd say, 'Yes, that's right, would you like a cup of tea?' I never could get into that.

GEORGE MICHAEL Andrew Ridgley and I had both just come from school about nine months before we took off with WHAM! Andrew was on the dole and I was doing two part-time jobs. In interviews though, I said I was on the dole because it was very trendy at the time to be on the dole as far as the music press was concerned. We then realized that we had to change that image, if you like to call it that, because we weren't really living normal lives any more. That was when we went into this wholesome, sun-tanned, high-gloss image. It worked and I think it was honest because we were filming in hot places.

PHIL COLLINS I've only ever had one job. I'm thirty-five and I've been playing drums for thirty years, almost. And in that time I really only ever had one proper job and that was for two weeks. The day I joined Genesis, they all went on holiday for two weeks, so there I was, with no money. My girlfriend at the time was the daughter of an exterior decorator, and I hated exterior decorating – I mean, even at home just helping out – I hated it, but I did it because it was something to do. And by the end of the two weeks I was just slapping paint here, there and everywhere and I painted over all the locks and things like that, because I didn't really care too much about it. But after a few weeks my girlfriend's dad got a phone call from the old couple we'd painted the house for, they wanted to get in the coal shed and couldn't because I'd painted over the lock. That was my one experience of a real job. I feel very lucky to be able to make a living doing what I want to do.

PAT PHOENIX It was a long time before I got the fame I was looking for. My marriage failed and I was doing about one job every six months – I was on the fringe of things. I didn't want to be dependent upon anybody, and I thought, 'This is the day to end it all,' but I didn't want to make anybody upset about it, so I put the cat out and I didn't leave a note and I thought, 'I'll make this look very natural.' So I put the gas on and I thought, 'Right, this is it ... I shall be no trouble to anybody.' About an hour later I woke up and there was a hell of a smell of gas and I was still there, and my friend came and said, 'There's an awful smell of gas in this flat, you'll kill yourself one of these days.' The shilling had run out, which was typical of me.

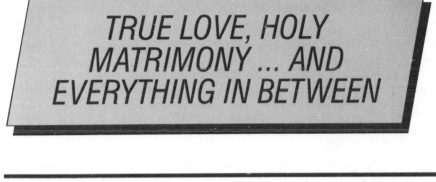

TRUE LOVE, HOLY MATRIMONY ... AND EVERYTHING IN BETWEEN

I don't really recommend being a bachelor – it's not really on, you know.
— Patrick Moore

Love, sex, marriage ... where would we be without them, and not necessarily in that order, either. I suppose you could say I was a something of a late developer in two out of three. My encounters with girls were destined always to end in rejection until I'd left my teens behind me. I caught up a bit during the '60s when I became the oldest teenager in town – in fact I was in my early thirties. As for love, I fell easily and often. I was lucky in that I didn't even have to know the women I worshipped, which opened the field up somewhat – I was happy to admire from afar. I think I had quite good taste. Elizabeth Taylor was my first love. Ann Sheridan I adored, and I was desperately fond of Deborah Kerr, but that was a pure love, unlike my feelings for Lauren Bacall, which were pure lust.

All I know is that love, falling in it and out of it, and everything in between, is a fascinating subject to me and to many of my guests. Let's start with the basic facts of life. . . .

PETER COOK I remember arriving at public school, and we were ushered into the housemaster's study, and he said, 'Well, sex is a thorny subject. You'll probably notice that all the boys at this school are boys, and all of the masters and staff are men – apart from Matron. But leaving Matron aside, you may notice that some of the older boys are half-boys and half-men. And some of you younger boys may have discovered that some of the older boys have become attached to you. You may have become attached to them, too, but don't, because sex is a precious gift from God. And like all gifts, it should not be unwrapped before its time, so don't unwrap your gift, or allow anyone else to unwrap your gift, or else God might, in His wisdom, come down and take it away again.' And I don't think any of us really picked up much from that.

PETER USTINOV I never knew anything about the facts of life – I didn't know until far too late. We had those Russian dolls where you unscrew one and there's another inside, and I thought people were born fully clothed.

FIONA FULLERTON I don't think I was told a great deal about the facts of life. My mother was a Calvinistic Methodist, so you can draw your own conclusions. I had to find out the hard way – to coin a phrase.

ARTHUR MARSHALL I was born in 1910 and my parents were therefore Victorian, and in those days you were told absolutely nothing. I knew nothing of the facts of life until I got to my preparatory school, when at the age of thirteen, all of the boys who were leaving were summoned to the headmaster's study. Of course, we all thought some terrible crime had been discovered, but along we went, and for once he was looking really quite genial. We were all asked to sit down – which was absolutely unheard of – and then he said, 'Well, I expect you've all been wondering how you got here . . .' Well, we hadn't been wondering at all, we'd come straight along the corridor, but of course he was speaking in a wider sense. And he said, 'You've got absolutely nothing to worry about because you see it's like this: when a lady and a gentleman love one another, there's a little thing that's provided by the gentleman and a little thing that's provided by the lady and the two little things meet up in the lady's cave and form a baby. Now, are there any questions?' Well, of course, we were full of questions but nobody dared to ask anything. However, the word 'thing' became a dreadful joke with us, particularly when we had the hymn 'All things bright and beautiful'. . . .

JOAN RIVERS My mother never told me the facts of life. I knew nothing, and that was horrendous. On my wedding night my husband said, 'I'm going to blow in your ear.' I said 'Use a kleenex.' I had never seen even a picture of a naked man. My husband walked over to the bathroom – I hung my blouse on it ... I said, 'This is great, he's going to support me *and* I've got somewhere to put my coat.'

TEENAGE OBSESSIONS....

BARRY NORMAN When I was about twelve, I was in love with Doris Day – and that was before she was a virgin! But I think it's permissible to be in love with Doris Day when you're twelve. After that I was crazy about Marilyn Monroe.

MEL BROOKS Sex was my motivation for getting into showbusiness – I thought I'd get some. When you're short and funny looking ... well, I knew that funny men are somehow sexually attractive and I danced my way into the hearts of many women. A lot of them had to go to the hospital, of course – if you dance your way into a human heart there's a lot of surgery that has to be done later. But you know, women are funny – in some ways they're really slightly hypocritical. For instance, when you're a teenager, you beg to go on a date and you beg and you say 'Please could we just kiss in the doorway? Could I touch?' 'No, no.' 'Could I hold ...?' 'Oh no, no,' they'd say, 'Oh no, I don't do that, I don't do it.' So anyway, finally one night they know you. They finally say all right, they succumb to it, they do it. . . . The next day, you say, 'Let's go to the cinema, let's go to the movies.' They say, 'No, let's do it.' You say, 'Let's have a piece of cake,' they say, 'Let's do it.' You say, 'Let's take a walk,' they say, 'I'd rather do it' – that's all they want to do, to do it!

CLIVE JAMES You only kissed in those days. When you were an adolescent in Sydney, Australia, in the '50s, kissing was as much as you hoped to achieve and even that was difficult. Very very few girls kissed, and the ones that did weren't necessarily the best kissers. In fact, a rule of life which I should have seen in its perfect clarity, was already operating. It is that the person who was best at doing something didn't want to do it – and the person who was available to do it wasn't good at it. The girl that did most of the kissing was the worst kisser, I won't say her name although I remember it well. There was a lot of spit and the teeth bumped into yours which meant that you were spitting chips of enamel afterwards, and she kissed with her eyes open and she had a very bad squint – so you always thought that she was watching something else.

None of my chat-up lines ever worked, probably because I learned them too early – I was heavily influenced by American television programmes of the '50s which we saw in Australia. Do you remember *77 Sunset Strip*? It starred this kid called Ed Byrnes and he sat in a Ford Thunderbird or Chevrolet and he combed his hair like this, and he said, 'Hi-ya chick, howd'ya like to take a three-hundred horse power plunge into the landscape?' And I used this line but it didn't sound so effective because I was sitting on a bicycle. In other words, you've got to have, shall we say, the equipment to go with the line.

BILLY CONNOLLY I was sexually avoidable. I thought I was OK, but I was all Old Spice and acne. I was a trendy thing, a lilac tie and hanky but the hanky was only a wee thing with three points and when you pulled it out it was a piece of paper. I said, 'What if I go out with Deborah Kerr, and she starts to cry? I can't go, "Here, darling, this is blotting paper...." ' I could dance but I couldn't turn corners. So I danced till we got to the edge of the room and then I danced right out the door and up the street.

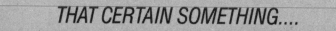

THAT CERTAIN SOMETHING....

OMAR SHARIF When I meet a girl, it takes me about two hours to eradicate the image she has of me – which is usually totally wrong – so that she gets to know me as I really am. But it can be very difficult if you have this reputation which makes them expect some tremendous lover performance from you – which you're not up to, really. You're so terrified of letting her down somehow, that's paralysing.

I was once in a motel in Dallas, Texas, and at four in the morning there was a knock on the door. I opened the door, and there was this lady who was obviously, visibly, drunk and she walked into the room and she said, 'I want to make love with you.' I said, 'Madam, you have to go out, it's four in the morning, I'm going to call security.' So she opened her bag and she took a gun out and she cocked it and she said, 'Take your clothes off.' She was drunk, as I say. And I did ... I took my clothes off, and she said, 'Everything'. So I went on, till I was stark naked and she lay on the bed, pulled her skirts up and said, 'Come and make love to me.' And I said, 'Madam, I would love to – but as you can see, I can't.'

TELLY SAVALAS Me a sex symbol? By nature I'm warm, I am sensitive, I'm affectionate, I cry a lot, but I was born ugly. The truth is, I'm a pussy cat, baby. If I'm a sex symbol, Michael, you do me a great favour and spread the word, baby!

DUDLEY MOORE All I can say is that being called a sex symbol is better than being called a haddock.

ALAN COREN It's very odd, but I find Margaret Thatcher enormously attractive – this may tell you much more about me than I really want you to know. But I've spent time in her presence and she's a very sexy lady. I think it's because she's got good legs.

DENIS HEALEY I think power gives people attraction – Henry Kissinger, who was not the most handsome man in the world, became absolutely overwhelmingly attractive to women when he became dominant, and he used to take out Hollywood starlets. I always remember him being asked why a chap with his responsibility spent his evenings with people like Jill St John and he replied, 'Well, if you spent the whole day with Indira Ghandi you don't want to spend the night with Golda Meir. . . .' I think power can be a bit of an aphrodisiac.

BOY GEORGE I once saw this great T-shirt in New York which said, 'If you love somebody let them go ... and if they don't come back, hunt them down and shoot them'. I definitely believe in love,

I'll do almost anything for love, even kill. I think it's important to everybody. When you initially meet somebody, you look at them and you decide whether you like what you see. On the other hand, if you're married to somebody for forty years and they get fat, you don't just divorce them because they get fat. I think people do underestimate what is sexually attractive. Often you see a beautiful girl with an ugly guy and people say 'Why is she with him?' or vice versa, but that person may have something that you'll never have.

PAYING COURT....

DUDLEY MOORE I remember taking a girl out once and I really did fancy her – oh, she was beautiful. We went to this very flash restaurant and I was really nervous, you know the feeling – anyway blood was rushing, and I was looking at the menu – my French is pretty good – and I thought I'd fancy a pork cutlet. But in fact, I hadn't ordered pork cutlet, I'd ordered pig's head. And this little piglet head came and sat down almost by itself. So there I am, during this rather romantic conversation, toying with the little hairs in it's ears, not knowing whether I should try and get in through the snout or what – but it had a happy ending.

BRIGITTE NEILSON It's perfectly true that I set out to 'catch' Sylvester Stallone. I've always believed that if you're determined about something, and go at it one hundred per cent, then you might be lucky. What happened was that I was in New York, and someone told me that Sylvester Stallone was in town. I said, 'Great, I'll go and talk to him. . . .' So this guy gave me the number of the hotel where Stallone was staying and I rang it, and the lady who answered the phone said, 'Look, there are three or four people on the line, would you like to hold?' And I said, 'Yes,' and I was holding and holding and nothing happened. I must have left ten or fifteen messages a day, and of course, why would he want to talk to me? In the end, I sent him a picture, and a letter, and I explained that I'd just finished my first film, and would like to talk to him. And soon the phone rang, and he said, 'This is Sylvester Stallone.' I said, 'Well, great,' and he said, 'Why did you do that?' I said, 'To be quite honest, I'd just like

Looks as if the joke's on me ... Norman Tebbit and John Cleese
seem to be having a good time though.

An all-theatrical line-up: Sir Michael Hordern, Dame Judi Dench
and Mr Alan Bates.

Telly Savalas, Felicity Kendall and Mike Yarwood.

Peter Cook, George Michael and his pin-up Jacqueline Bisset.

to talk to you.' And he came over and we talked, and then he left. Then he called me and said, 'Why don't you come to dinner?' so I went to dinner, and one thing led to another. . . .

BARRY MANILOW What approach do I use with girls? I do what any other horny person would do. I would call, I would beg, send her free tickets, anything.

HARRY SECOMBE I'd been out the army about three days and I went to this dance with some army mates. I didn't have my glasses on but I picked up this little dark pretty bird. I was dancing with her and we made a date for the following day outside the Plaza cinema at six o'clock. But of course I'd had a few drinks, and I hadn't worn my glasses anyway, so when the time came to meet her I wasn't quite sure what she looked like. The Plaza cinema had columns outside it, so I got there at ten to six, got behind the pillar and thought, 'If I don't fancy her when I see her, I won't come out.' And I waited behind there till quarter past six and thought she wasn't coming, and so I got out from behind the pillar . . . and she got out from behind hers!

MASCULINE, FEMININE

LES DAWSON W.C. Fields used one phrase which I've always loved – especially after all the years I've been married – he said, 'Elephants are just like women – nice to look at, but who wants to own one?'

STEWART GRANGER I tried to be a good husband. My only alibi is that all my wives had contact with me three years before they married me so they knew what they were getting into. I didn't sweep them off their feet – we sort of lived together. Well, we didn't live together in those days because it wasn't thought proper. We sort of did it and went home! I think God's big joke is that he put men and women together. We both desire each other and torture each other, we can't live with each other, and we can't live without each other.

LAUREN BACALL My definition of a real man is someone who knows who he is, knows what he's all about. Someone who's not two years old, or has to be catered to and taken care of . . . You don't have to be a star, you don't have to be rich, you just have to know what you're about, you have to have a point of view in life, and what I'm interested in more than anything else, is an exchange, being able to talk to somebody. And I can tell you something, I don't want to talk about *them* all the time. I don't want to talk about me either, but just be what you are.

GERMAINE GREER I sometimes think the people who write to agony aunts are really sort of boasting – 'I have seven men in love with me' and all that, you know. 'My husband won't leave me alone' – he will, don't worry honey, he will.

Men are very important to me – one cleaned out the gutters while I was away, and Cecil looks after the garden. No, they are very important to me. I see a few of them every day, I live amongst them, I treat them generally with courtesy. But what I would really like, is a very small man who will do the books for me. A very small, silent, perhaps deaf man. I've got a space for him under the stairs, I could make it quite comfortable.

ZSA ZSA GABOR I can live without luxury. But love is essential to me. I don't like the feminists. I think a woman should be feminine and a man should be a man, and I must have a man who tells me what to do. I don't believe a man is ever used – only women are used. And they always have been because women are the nice little sweethearts who stay at home and cook. You read about the American scandals with all these famous politicians who have an affair with their secretary in the office, while the poor little wife is at home, looking after the children and the husband. But I make sure I don't slave too much. I never liked housework – in fact, believe it or not, I still don't know how to vacuum. I can cook, but I still can't make a bed – for the simple reason that it breaks my fingernails. There is no better husband than one who does the housework.

OMAR SHARIF I would like to have been born a woman – I actually think a lot more of women than men. Men are children, they never grow up, they're always four or five years old. I've never met a man who is really an adult. Girls are born adults – you see a little girl, a two-year-old girl, she puts her arms around you and says: 'Oh, I love you, Daddy, you're so wonderful, can I have this please?' Little boys stamp their feet and say, 'I want this!' He can't work out that he's got to be more diplomatic, more clever. Little girls are born with that instinct – they know straight away how to deal with their mums and dads and everybody.

THE TENDER TRAP....

KELLY MONTEITH I didn't get married until relatively late. I had to learn how to compromise. I always wanted to find a woman who liked to do what I liked to do – but I could never find one who wanted to drink and chase women.

JOAN COLLINS I was brought up in a generation where there were only two kinds of girls – girls who did and girls who didn't. Nice girls saved everything until they were married and bad girls, well, bad girls did the opposite. And so I decided that this was rather an unfair situation – why shouldn't women be able to do what a man did? But of course it doesn't really work like that.

I don't know about marrying again – I think it's a bit doubtful. But as for meeting somebody with whom you could be together, well, I wouldn't say no to that. . . . I think when you've been once burnt – or in my case, four times burnt – then you have to be a bit careful. But I didn't get married four times because I like trolling down the aisle, I got married four times because I like the idea of being married and I like sharing my life with a man. I think it's wonderful – if it works. And if it doesn't work, then I think that you just have to end it. I just don't want to ever make any more mistakes again. And I hope I don't – touch wood!

SARAH BRIGHTMAN I was auditioning for *Cats* and that's where I really first met Andrew Lloyd Webber. I remember the first day I met him. I went for an audition to his flat, and I took along my little piece of paper and music score and everything. And I remember walking in the door and he was looking at me, and I thought, 'Gosh, what's the matter?' because he was just staring at me. Of course, at the time I was a punk and I had all this blue hair and everything and he must have thought, 'My God, who is this strange girl?' I remember I sang terribly, and he played rather badly, but in fact we ended up singing 'Don't Cry For Me, Argentina' and it was fine. And I ended up being in *Cats* and then, a year-and-a-half later, marrying him. But it wasn't love at first sight. . . . I thought he was rather a funny man and he thought I was rather a funny girl.

DAVID FROST Many years ago – back in the early '70s, I think – Burt Reynolds called up Warren Beatty and me and formed Marriage Anonymous on the theory that if any of the three of us got tempted to get married we'd ring up the others and we'd go round and make them drunk.

LAUREN BACALL I was 19 years old when I made *To Have and To Hold*, but Humphrey Bogart was never my idol. Howard Hawks, who owned my contract, always said that he wanted to put me in a film with either Bogie, or Cary Grant, and I always thought, 'Oh, Cary Grant, naturally, how great that would be.' But Howard decided on Bogart. Many actors would not have accepted me – after all I'd never made a film before. But I remember I was on the way into Howard's bungalow, and Bogie was coming out, having just seen my screen test, and he said, 'We're going to have a lot of fun together.' And we did. . . .

Bogie wouldn't have married me if I hadn't been prepared to agree not to follow my career. In other words, if I was going to go on location and disappear from home for six months at a time, forget it. He said, 'Listen, I've been married to three actresses and if you want a career, I will send you merrily on your way. I will always love you, but I don't want to be married to someone who's not going to be with me – that's not what marriage is all about.' And I agreed with him. Actually I was so anxious to have him that I would have said anything – but I did put my marriage first, I made that choice, and although it meant I had many, many years of frustration as an actress, I'm not sorry I made that choice. I think it was the right one.

Of course, I was devastated when Bogie died. I think I was in a semi-coma all the time. It's not something you ever get over, and I don't really want to get over it. I don't want to forget him – I couldn't forget him, he was too big a part of my life and much too important to me. But of course I think about him in a much different way as the years go by, and now I always smile when I think of him, because he made me laugh. Whenever Bogie was at a party, that was where the fun was. He was just a very extraordinary man and I was very fortunate to have had those twelve years. I've not had anything close to twelve years like it, since, I can tell you!

JUDI DENCH It wasn't love at first sight when I met Michael [Williams] – it was good friends at first sight, though, for nine years. And then, suddenly, it was love. I was working in Australia, and he flew out with his last penny, and without telling me he was coming, to pop the question. He chose a wonderful day, a really glorious day, and we were going for a picnic, there were blue skies and white sand, and he asked me to marry him. It was too perfect. I thought, 'This won't last when we're in Soho on a wet day,' so I said, 'I think you'd better wait. Don't ask me now, ask me on a rainy day in London.'

People who knew us well before we married didn't think there was a chance of it working. He is Cancerian and I'm a Sagittarian and he describes it as him rushing towards the dark, and me rushing towards the light, and we both drag each other back, into a kind of middle earth. A lot of people say, 'How on earth can you manage to work together in the theatre, and then come home and be together, too?' But it's always been that way. The first year we were married, we were at Stratford, and in nearly every play together. It just seemed to form the basis of how it was going to be.

NEIL KINNOCK We had a Debating Society in school which was pretty tough – if you dropped clangers, missed the point or otherwise made a clown of yourself, it was remembered throughout the following week until you had a chance to redeem yourself. But when I went to university, I didn't bother at all until I encountered a girl who I got the impression would be immensely impressed if I could speak. So in order to impress her I made a speech and it apparently *did* impress her because I'm married to her now. That was the strict reason I did it, because I hadn't bothered before – I thought debates were boring.

Glenys is really a strong critic, she tells me the truth, that's the most important thing, because it simply wouldn't be any good living with a fan who said that everything you did was absolutely fine and perfect and wonderful, because nothing would have validity. So when Glenys says it's good, it was pretty good, and when she doesn't say it was good, it was pretty bad. . . . I think our marriage is pretty normal. There are areas of contention – I can't really think of any at the moment – but I'll tell you I am in extremely good books at the moment, because I cooked Christmas lunch. Glenys was ill, she had this 'flu that was going around. We had nine people for Christmas lunch – my mother and father-in-law came down from Anglesey and the kids and Glenys and myself and some friends. And I cooked this superb lunch. She sat on a stool in the kitchen and gave orders like an admiral, you know, and it was wonderful. I've never ever attempted anything like that in my life before. Not only was it edible, it was superb, we should've captured it on camera. I couldn't get over the fact that it was so good. And I'm very neat about things, so everything was in line, I had seven vegetables and it was piping hot, it really was, I'm going to say it again – it was superb. It was a great achievement and I said to her, 'How was it so good?' And she said, 'Because you must be the only person in Britain who cooked Christmas lunch today and did nothing else at all.' I realized that I hadn't moved two feet away from the oven all morning, and I was exhausted. How people do it I don't know.

ZSA ZSA GABOR Romance is very important because it keeps you happy and alive. I'm the stupidest woman in the world as far as romance goes. But when a man starts to look around, and look at other women, that's when I leave because I don't want to suffer. Why should I suffer for a man when there are so many in the world? I just don't want to go through having a man say, 'Well, darling, I have to stay late in the office,' or 'I have to stay on the polo field.' That's when a woman should end it. It's lucky when you have a husband or a wife for a whole lifetime. I don't know why I always marry my men – it must be some kind of phobia. I'm so accustomed to being married that I cannot be unmarried. It's the look on the maid's face in the morning when she brings in breakfast and there's a man in your bed and you can say, 'That's my husband.'

DOLLY PARTON I met my husband the first day I went to Nashville, in 1964, and we've been together ever since. We've become great friends – he respects what I do. He likes to be very private. He's with me more than the Press would lead you to believe, but they never see him so they assume we're never together. He just doesn't like the limelight. In his way, he's my country boy – he's very sweet and romantic – he writes me poems occasionally. He's very kind and very good to me and I've never doubted his love and he's never doubted mine. It's my first marriage and his first marriage and until one of us dies, that's the way it's going to be.

IAN BOTHAM I rely on Kathy totally. What we've been through in the last few years has brought us a lot closer, and that's part of the reason I'm getting out of the rat race of international cricket ... certainly for a few years, anyway. Kath and the children are the most important things in my life now, whereas for years I think cricket was. And when they banned me from playing cricket for a month, they actually did me a favour. I spent a month at home with the children and I suddenly realized all the things that I was missing out on – watching the baby grow up, start to crawl, the first few words, things like that. Whereas before I'd be home for perhaps two hours and then away for five months, now I appreciate that there's a lot more to life.

MARGARET THATCHER My husband take a back seat? Oh my dear, he doesn't. Why should he – he has his own career, his own life and he's pretty forthright on many things – and a very good thing, too. He does a lot of work, and he does a lot for many charities, for example The Sports Aid Foundation. For him, rugby football is an absolute religion, so he goes out and he does his own thing, and my goodness he says some forthright things, too – marvellous!

YOKO ONO I'd heard about Elvis Presley and also I'd heard about the Beatles as a social phenomenon and I remembered the name Ringo because Ringo means apple in Japan. But when John and I first met nobody warned me that it was him, and so I just didn't know who he was, but I thought he was very sort of gentle and clean cut, a nice sort of person. What happened was that John was with these three very interesting, exciting people – Paul, George and Ringo and now it was just going to be me. I had to fill this space of three people and more. He burned the bridge to that whole world and came to me, so you see, it was quite a heavy responsibility. I know I'm criticized for splitting up with John, but in fact I had to. Somehow it was healthier for us to be separated at the time.

In my case, the minute I got together with John I lost an audience because I'm an artist and it was very important for me to work, and keep on expressing myself, and have an audience. But the minute I became Mrs Lennon, that was over. Also the whole world was wishing we would split, saying 'Oh, she's got a hold on him' and, so part of me was saying, 'OK, here, take it.'

We got back together at Elton John's concert, where John was also performing. I wasn't going to go, but this gallery owner asked me to take him so we went to the concert, and John came out at the end and sang a few songs and the applause was incredible – the whole house was shaking and he was bowing when they were applauding. But he bowed just one too many times, and I thought, 'Oh, he must be feeling insecure.' And I just saw the lonely John up there on the stage. He was never like that when he was with me. And I thought, 'Did I do that to him?' I felt very guilty, and when I went backstage, we looked at each other – and the rest is history . . .

BRITT EKLAND I was twenty-one when I met Peter Sellers. I remember when I married him but I don't remember when I met him, although I know it was just ten days between the two occasions. He was a very tormented man, I know that now, but at the time I didn't understand it, and so it was a very tormented relationship. I was twenty-one, I had just come out of Sweden and my eyes were like saucers. I thought, 'Here is this man who just begs to be loved, and who just wants to be a handsome, gorgeous leading man,' but who really was not. I mean, he was a comic genius, yet he still wanted to be something he wasn't.

BOB NEWHART I've been married for twenty-two years. My wife – I had the good fortune to marry a woman – she's kept me very level. Whenever I started to get carried away she would say, 'Look, you're not that great, you know', which is good. She's rather an unusual woman. She tends to talk to the actors on the screen at the movies. We went to see *Papillon* with Steve McQueen and Dustin Hoffman, about Devil's Island, and they were taking him into Devil's Island, and they announced that if you tried to escape, that was all right. They'd pick you up and put you in the hole for two years, but if you tried to escape with a gun, they would kill you. So the movie went on and Steve McQueen and Dustin Hoffman plotted this escape and McQueen took this gun and my wife stood up in the middle of this crowded theatre and yelled out, 'They said don't take the gun!'

People on either side of me turned round and I pretended I wasn't with her.

TOM JONES My wife does try to keep me in check. She tries to get me to do things around the house, like changing light bulbs and things like that. It keeps your feet on the ground, I think. For me it was a good thing to get married young because by the time I got into show business the marriage was already solid. We grew up together, we went to school together and that was it. And it wasn't a shock when I got my first hit record because I was trying for that all our lives and so she backed me all the way. Well to me, being on stage is the closest thing to actually making love, you know. I mean it's the same kind of adrenalin.

EXTRAMARITALLY SPEAKING....

ROGER MOORE My wife, Louisa, is Italian, and as you know, Italians are never jealous! I'd go off to work, and she'd look at the script and say: 'Who are you working with today, what are you doing?' And I'd say, 'Well, I wouldn't come to the studio today, because I have to be in bed with so and so.' And she'd say, 'All right, I understand you have to do this – just don't enjoy it!'

CHUCK BERRY Can you imagine a man killing another man because that other man gave his wife pleasure? You know, it's not worth death. If people stopped to think, there wouldn't be so much jealousy.

> *Aspel:* If this were your own situation with your lovely wife, would you kill?
> *Chuck:* No – but I would surely educate him, you know.

GEORGE MELLY I remember once I was on the steps of a hotel in Liverpool, and a middle-aged woman wearing a maroon coat came up and said, 'Hey, George, you know I've always loved you, could I have your autograph?' So I signed, and then she said something that rocked me back on my heels. She said, 'There's only two men I'd commit adultery with right off – you and Frankie Vaughan.' And I had this strange image of myself and Frankie Vaughan sitting in her front room, spinning a coin to see who went first.

LOVE SCENES....

JENNY AGUTTER Love scenes in the movies are never as romantic as they seem. They always choose spots which sound wonderful, like beaches or haystacks or something, which in real life are extremely uncomfortable and not very nice to be in at all. Or if they do manage to put you in a bedroom, remember that you've got a whole camera team there, and they usually want to do some extraordinary shot from very close up, so they put you right on the edge of the bed, probably on a board which you're about to fall off at any minute. And the other actor you're playing with has probably got drunk so he'll be able to relax and feel comfortable with the scene, so you're also trying to avoid the fumes of the alcohol. It's not very romantic.

STEWART GRANGER Copulating is not a pretty exercise – it's not pretty to look at. In films back in my day, you suggested it – you disappeared, and panned off on to two doves cooing or something, and you *imagined* it. You know, I used to play romantic parts but never once did I open my mouth when I kissed, although I think I kissed rather passionately on screen. But people like Richard Gere, they don't kiss, they eat, they virtually have a meal. You can actually see their tongue!

MICHAEL CAINE The most difficult thing I ever had to do in the cinema was to kiss Christopher Reeve. I said to him: 'If you open your mouth, I'll kill you!' We prepared ourselves for the experience by drinking half a bottle of brandy each – I was worried about him until then. It really wasn't a happy day. For a start, Christopher's taller than I am so I was the fluffy one ... There was only one take. Bombed as we were, we got that sonofabitch right the first time, I'll tell you.

CHRISTOPHER REEVE I kissed Michael Caine.... We call that The Ten Million Dollar Kiss, and the reason was that that's about what it cost at the box office when people saw it. They just weren't ready. I'd just done *Superman 2* and they weren't prepared for the idea of Superman kissing another man. The fact that I was playing a psychotic homosexual didn't really seem to matter. They just couldn't take it. I tell you, we did it in one take – all the photographers were banned from the set and both my girlfriend and Michael Caine's wife were there, supervising things. And Michael said, 'If you close your eyes and lift your foot up, I'll know you're in love.'

DUSTIN HOFFMAN I never got to be as attractive as I wanted to be in *Tootsie*. We all agreed that we wouldn't make the film until I looked like a woman – the idea was the audience shouldn't have to suspend their disbelief. And sure enough it came the time where they were doing screen tests and the projectionist was saying: 'Who *is* she, who is that new actress?' I went down and talked to my daughter's teachers in school and she said, 'Daddy, get *out* of here, get out....' I said, 'Introduce me, say I'm your aunt.' It was like a trip – as a matter of fact, we were shooting on 57th Street, and at lunch time I would always walk out on the street. I just joined the crowd, and somebody said to me, 'Do you want to see where Woody Allen's offices are?' So we went up there and Woody Allen had just done a movie that José Ferrer was in, and José was there picking up the cheque I guess, and the assistant director I was with introduced me to him in the elevator: 'Mr Ferrer, this is Dorothy Michaelson.' We're in the elevator and the lighting isn't good there, it's dark. And he said, 'How do you do?' and I said, 'Oh, you're one of my favourite actors.' I did the whole thing – I said, 'I'm from Dallas and I do the theatre there but you're wonderful,' and everything like that. He said, 'Thank you, thank you....' I said, 'In fact, I think you're very sexy,' and I started getting carried away, you know, that kind of devilish side of me, and finally, just before the elevator hit the main floor, I said, 'How would you like to have your pipes cleaned, Mr Ferrer?' which is a kind of vulgar expression. And his face dropped and he just said, 'Not right now, thank you.' I walked out on the street and the Assistant Director told me later that José said, 'Who *was* that scumbag of a woman!'

FAME AND FORTUNE

Fame? Fame is never having to say you're sorry! It's been said before that being well-known is a double-edged sword. Sometimes it's nice to be recognized, and it's all right with me when people shout, 'Hello Mike!' But there are just as many times when it would be nice to be anonymous. Sometimes people are rude to you, just because they know your face. Or they can be over-generous in an embarrassing way: I've seen my wife offered the choice of a better cut of meat in a butcher's shop, when there are little old ladies queueing up. On the other hand, when you go abroad to a country where you're completely unrecognized, you're reminded what it's like to be a member of the public, and that can be very sobering – life without the smiles and knowing looks.

It's reasonable to suppose that people go into this business in search of fame. That wasn't the case with me, I just wanted the opportunity to do something that I knew I *could* do. That was all I wanted, not to climb into a white Rolls-Royce and wave to fans at premières and all that. But if you are well known, it seems foolish to pretend otherwise. I can never see why people refuse to give autographs, for example – it puts such a dampener on things. I saw it happen once to a dear old woman who went around a group of people, gently offering her book, and everyone signed except one. He said, 'No, I don't.' And she offered the book again, and he said, 'Why don't you go away and do something intelligent like read a book.' It was unforgivable. Perhaps it's an attempt to pretend that fame is worthless and spurious and all those things. Well, yes, we all know that, but if it gives the autograph seeker pleasure and it takes only a moment of your time, then it seems pointless not to oblige.

When I look back, it's impossible to pin-point a moment when it hit me that I was 'successful'. It took me a very long time because I don't have the kind of face which people immediately commit to memory, but if you keep popping up for thirty-five years, then inevitably people are going to say, 'Don't I know you?' There are times when you can feel successful when you've done virtually nothing – I remember when I became a radio actor, and I was pushing my motor bike, which had run out of petrol, up the main street in Cardiff, and I felt that I was a great star, and was very pleased with myself. I suppose it usually hits home when you see your name in print. I once played James 'Rocky' Mountain of the FBI in a 'Children's Hour' programme, and when I saw my name in the *Radio Times* I just stared at it for ages. I thought, 'This name looks good in print,' and that was quite a relief because Aspel is not a good name to pronounce – people always want to say Aspirin or Cesspool.... Something like Baker is much more sensible.

There are two other points about celebrity. One is that along with being spoilt and all those nice things, it also makes you a target for being used and taken advantage of. As one famous sportsman put it, 'Agree to do something for nothing and they'll tell you where the bus stop is; ask to be paid and they'll send the limo.' I was once asked by an ex-Director General of the BBC to open a fête. It was about a 70-mile drive away, if not more, and I went up there and was given a drink and introduced to a few people, and then I opened the fête ... and never saw anyone again. I was called 'Aspel' throughout, which should have prepared me.

Another time I passed a colleague in the corridor, and he asked if I'd like to go to his wedding. 'Fine,' I said. 'Will you be best man?' he asked, and I was a bit taken aback, but agreed anyhow. On the wedding day, he was holding his head and nudging his friends about the wild stag night they'd enjoyed. As I hadn't been invited to that, I had to conclude that I was there to work, wearing my professional hat. As a wedding present, I waived my normal fee.

The other thing about celebrity, of course, is that it can earn you a decent living – although usually only after years of struggle, as with most jobs. I've always said that money itself isn't important to me –

but I've still got young children and I'll always have to provide. It's all relative. As a child, money was tight. We never starved and we were healthy kids but we didn't get any pocket money, there was none to spare.

During the war when I was evacuated, I used to do a paper round. Then, when the shop stopped delivering, I thought I'd show a bit of private enterprise. I went to all the customers and offered to carry on delivering for threepence a week. It worked rather well, and I made far more by doing that than I ever had working for the paper shop. When it was time to go back to London, Auntie Rose – my 'mother' for four-and-a-half years – had saved up all my threepenny bits. They amounted to the grand sum of twelve pounds and ten shillings – a fortune! I was 11 years old and had money to burn. I spent it on a bike, carried on doing a paper round, and by the time I was 14, I was already contributing to the family coffers.

Later on, when I was living in Cardiff, I would often miss the last bus from my girlfriend's house and she used to lend me her bicycle. Pedalling home, I used to play a game – that with every light I saw on in a house, I would get £1,000 a year. Sometimes I'd get home earning £200,000 a year. It was a good game. In recent years, it's been nice to know that I could decide to take my wife Lizzie on Concorde and not have to ask permission from the bank manager, but I've never really gone in for extravagances – they all add up to too many paper rounds.

Most of my guests enjoy their fame, but they have discovered that, enjoyable though the trappings of celebrity may be, there is a price to be paid. . . .

TONY CURTIS I came out of a place where I had no money, and I learned at a very early age that what gives us our individual character and strength is economic solidity. If you've got a bank book or a few quid in your kip you've got it made. . . . It doesn't necessarily make you happy but it certainly makes you feel better than if you didn't have money.

BOY GEORGE Being wealthy is easier to handle than being poor. I came from a pretty poorish background and now it's nice to be able to give my parents money, and let them do things like go on holiday. That's the nice thing about being rich – especially when you've gone without because then you really appreciate it when you've got it.

BARRY McGUIGAN When I fight, I never think of being hurt – the one thing I fear is losing everything I've worked for – the security for the future, for the kids and everything. I'm afraid of losing that but not of simply losing, or getting hurt.

STEVE DAVIS Everybody says, 'Oh, you won £44,000 in the world championships, you must've been really pleased with that,' but it's not just the money, it's being able to pick up the trophy at the end – that's the nice thing.

CLAIRE RAYNER I blush to say this, but the number of books I've written is hovering around the seventy mark. I've been doing roughly three a year since I started writing and that's twenty-five years. Some of them are quite little books – some of them are enormous, mind you. Half of it's fiction. Frankly, that's what puts the jam on the bread. It's not dealing with problems. I'd hate anyone to think that I did well out of dealing with the problem page. That's me doing what I was trained to do, but the novels are fun. Thank God they make money.

KIRK DOUGLAS I've always tried to prepare for a role. When I did a detective story I worked for about a month in the 42nd Street precinct. One day I was in there working, and I was finger-printing a criminal, but he kept looking at me as I was doing it. In the end, he said, 'You're Kirk Douglas.' I said, 'If I was Kirk Douglas, with all his money, would I be here doing this?'

OMAR SHARIF I did a film in Las Vegas about five years ago, and I was gambling all the time. I sat at the gaming tables and said to the assistant director, you just call me when you're ready. I used to go and do the shot, and then go back and gamble. When the film was finished, I introduced the cashier to the producer of the film and I said to the producer, 'You know the money you owe me? Well, you don't owe it to me, you owe it to him', and pointed towards the cashier. I'd lost my entire salary, the whole lot. But I didn't care because I was earning money easily. I was looking for excitement because I was bored with my work, and the parts I was playing, and the films I was making. I suppose I was going through the male menopause, and I got through it with sheer will power. It was a case of either letting myself become a bum and gamble and lead a dissolute life, or getting a hold of myself and doing something positive about it.

STING I tend to live a normal life. I go to the pub. I go to the betting shop and people say, 'Hello Sting,' or 'I don't like you,' or whatever, but they talk to me. Occasionally, people act very strangely – I was driving down Edgware Road once and a taxi driver pulled up by me, and said, 'Sting! You've got a flat tyre,' and then he drove off. So I pulled to the side and I hadn't changed a tyre for a long time, but I got the jack out of the back and started to jack the car up, and while I was doing it, these two ladies went, 'Ah, it's Sting'. Then I got the nuts off, by which time these two ladies had become a crowd of people staring at me changing this tyre, and then it becomes a *performance*. You know, a lot of macho men are standing there going, 'Go on, Sting, can you do this?' So I got the tyre off, and I got the spare on, and put the nuts on, and at the end of it, I gave a bow, and they gave me a round of applause. I'm just so glad I could do it!

GEORGE MICHAEL Basically I don't spend money on anything but my profession. I love being able to put money back into what I do. I think more than anything I enjoy the freedom and there are two things in life that give you freedom. One is success in your own particular field, and the other is money. I've got no real regard for money, beyond security and comfort. I'm really not a great buyer – if I can't wear it and I can't eat it, then I'm not that bothered. I'm not trying to sound humble, but I've got a small house because it's all I need.

MICHAEL CAINE The lean times seemed very hard, but the thing you think of when you have some success is how on earth did you survive them? I suppose you survive them by not knowing anything else. If you start at the bottom there's nowhere to go down. The worst thing would be to go backwards, suddenly to go broke. I suppose if I went broke, I'd just start working all over again.

DENNIS WATERMAN One of my friends was at Sherborne and speaks very posh – I took him back to my place for a drink one day and my dad was going, 'Dennis, listen to Tim, listen – go on, talk, say something' and my friend says, 'Well I don't know what to say really, Mr Waterman,' and my dad says to me, 'Why don't you talk like that, you could make a fortune.' And Tim ever since has been going, 'If only I could be a cockney, Dennis, I would have made a fortune like you.'

THE TRAPPINGS OF FAME...

DAVID ESSEX A friend and I were in the back streets of St Tropez, looking for a taxi, and I was desperate for a pee. So I did – and all of a sudden a man with a gun grabbed me round the neck and dragged me off. I was still half-undressed! Apparently I'd chosen to pee up against a police station, so they took me inside, and told me off, and of course I apologized. And then the policeman said: 'We'll let you off on one condition.' 'What's that?' I said. And he said: 'You sign copies of "America"' – which was number one in France at the time! So being famous can be useful sometimes. . . .

CHARLTON HESTON I would say the advantages of success outweigh the disadvantages. Obviously there are pressures. You can't go to football games and things like that. But on the other hand you can always get a seat in an aeroplane and a table in a restaurant. I guess I've been a public person most of my life now and you get used to it.

JULIE CHRISTIE One of the things that's left over from school is an absolute terror of hearing my name pronounced in public. In fact when you introduced me, I thought, 'Oh my God, I'm going to be brought up in front of the assembly for some heinous crime and be humiliated.' And that was, I think, the feeling when I got the Oscar – 'I've got to go up there, what am I going to do?' I think I burst into tears, to my shame.

GLENDA JACKSON Awards are nice for the day, and they glitter – my mother has got all mine and she polishes them within an inch of their lives, she's polished all the gold glitter away and it's base metal underneath, and I think that's a fairly apt analogy of what a prize is. They are nice for the day, but they don't mean anything, they don't make you any better. And what irritates me about them more than anything is the artificial device that actors somehow compete one with the other for the prize. The actors have the least to do with those things – somebody else enters you, they almost run the race for you. You have absolutely nothing at all to do with it, and I resent sometimes the implications that there is this kind of artificial competitiveness amongst actors, because it's been my experience that it doesn't exist. There are few really good parts knocking around and it's the parts that get the award more than the performances, I think. And we really are not out to kill each other in the way that quite often those awards would lead one to believe.

I felt truly honoured to be asked on *The Morecambe and Wise Show* and I still do – I regard my appearance with them as the apotheosis of my career and I don't say that lightly or gratuitously. It was a genuine privilege to work with them because you could be the richest person in the world and then some, and still not be able to buy the experience that they carried within them. My second Oscar was entirely due to Morecambe and Wise and they sent me a telegram to prove it: 'Stick with us and we'll get you a third', I think it was.

THE PRICE OF FAME...

GEORGE HARRISON I think the mania got to me in about 1966 and around that time I got a bit tired of what they call the adulation. I'm still not keen on that side of it – it's nice to be popular, it's nice to be loved, but it's not so nice to be chased round and to be on the front page of the paper every day of your life, with people climbing over the wall all day long.

TERRY JONES *The Sun* had all sorts of details about my private life that I never knew about. For example, it said I had a daughter called Samantha (which is not true), and it said that I had a Citroen car (which I don't – I drive a Renault) and that I spent three years at the Royal College of Art painting ten-inch red stripes on a piece of canvas and then it quoted me and it said: ' "I don't know why we did it," says Terry. "It was a complete waste of time." ' Well, none of it is true – I've never been to the Royal College of Art – or any college of art for that matter. But I got my own back – at the time I was writing a column for the *Guardian*, so I wrote '20 Things You Didn't Know About the Editor of *The Sun*' – the Editor of *The Sun* wears his pyjamas over his head and he has twelve daughters, all called Spot.

CLIFF RICHARD I don't mind what people say about me any more. I think that people like us are up for grabs anyway. We're public figures and so therefore we know we're in the firing line. I just think to myself, 'Well, I've survived twenty-six years of this, I'll manage another twenty-six. . . .'

Once a girl sort of posted herself to me. She put herself in a box and got someone to deliver her. I thought someone'd given me a TV set – I was so excited, I ripped the box open and this girl went, 'Can I have your autograph?'

JULIO IGLESIAS Sometimes you wake up in the morning and you read something about yourself and you say, 'My God, this isn't true!' – but it's good because it's on the front page, and we love it.

LULU Like most people, the time that I'm least able to control my temper is in the car. If I'm cutting somebody up they should just let me cut them up. They should not get annoyed, because if they shout or beep, I start shouting obscenities. But then I see them point at me, and go, 'Lulu!' and I think, 'Oh God, they'll turn off next time I'm on the telly!'

SEBASTIAN COE I think you probably need an element of nastiness somewhere if you're going to be a winner . . . you have to want to be the best. I think that's the one thing. It's getting there without trampling on too many people. I've tried, but it's not always been easy. There have been times when in order to maintain that kind of standard, you had to do things that haven't been particularly popular.

WHAT'S IN A NAME?

CLIFF RICHARD As soon as I chose the name Cliff Richard I came home, told the family, and they said, 'All right, Cliff.' From then onwards, the only one who used to make a little mistake every now and then was my little sister, who'd say Harry and then quickly change it to Cliff. They've never called me Harry since that time. In fact now, when people think they're really being smart, they phone up stage doors and say, 'Can I speak to my brother Harry?' But I know it's totally untrue because none of my sisters or my mother would ever call me Harry again.

LENNY HENRY My real name is Lenworth. Lenworth George Henry. My mum must have had a seizure of something when she had me – 'Let's call him Lenworth!'

LORETTA SWIT Would I give myself a name like this? If I stayed up all night, no! It means 'dawn' in Polish – which is what I am.

LULU Listen, my real name is Marie McDonald McClaughlin Laurie. With my name on the front of the theatre, nobody else would get a chance. I think I'll stick with Lulu – I'm not superstitious but it's been so good for me up until now that I'm not going to throw it away.

KIRI TE KANAWA Someone said the name Kiri means bell, but I really think it means 'skin' – 'skin of a tree'. I always chose the prettiest version of it.

SIGOURNEY WEAVER I was christened Susan but for some reason I thought I was too tall for the name – I was already 5 feet 10 inches when I was 12 years old. So I just took Sigourney out of a book by F. Scott Fitzgerald and I don't know how, or why, but I just kept it.

SUCCESS ... A PERSONAL VIEW....

PAT PHOENIX Many years ago when I was in a play with Thora Hird she presented us all at the end of the show with a bottle of champagne. I tucked mine under my arm and she said, 'Aren't you gonna drink it?' and I said, 'No, I'll drink it when I make it', and it's still on the top of my wardrobe, waiting to be opened. Because I think success is when you satisfy yourself. No matter how they cheer, or what they do, when you do that one thing that you've always wanted to do, that's when you're a success. It's not in other people's eyes.

MICHAEL HORDERN I had a fishing fly named after me. I tied a fly which was extremely successful and it was called Hordern Pheasant Tail Nymph. And Hardy's were probably the best known fishing tackle shop in the world and it got into the hands of one of the Hardy's brothers and he said, 'May we market it under your name?' and I said, 'My God, I'd rather have that than a knighthood' – this was some years ago – and then Hardy's were rationalized, which means of course that everything costs twice as much and there wasn't as much in the shop. And my fly came out of that catalogue. When it disappeared from the catalogue and by chance I was offered a knighthood, I always said that the Queen, coming as she does from an angling family, was compensating me for having had my name taken out of Hardy's catalogue.

MARGARET THATCHER Let me put it this way, I'm doing the one job in the world which I really want to do, which I love – and work to me is pleasure, so I don't have very much time and even the things I do in a way are relaxation. If I have to read things up, this is a relaxation – I love music, I love gardening and I love just pottering round the house. Now for a housewife that's a bore, for me, it is a relaxation. If I've got to turn out drawers or turn out the airing cupboard or get the kitchen tidy, it's a relaxation for me and I like it, or just going through some interior decoration books or moving the furniture round – I'm a great mover of furniture.

DAME EDNA EVERAGE I'm not plugging anything, I'm not selling a book or a hit record. I'm just here. I'm just giving of myself. I can't understand it sometimes. My tax lawyers, they ring me up, they say, 'What the dickens are you doing the Aspel show for?' and I say, 'I'm sorry, I've got so much to give, so much to share.'

NO TURN UNSTONED

We had a good letter once, it said, 'Dear Eric Morecambe, you can't sing, you can't dance, and you can't tell jokes and you're not funny. PS. Get rid of your partner – he's dragging you down.'

– Ernie Wise

It's a fact of life that if you're in any way well known, then you're going to come in for criticism. It's also a fact of life that it hurts and if anybody says it doesn't, I don't believe them. Most performers can read ten glowing reports and one bad, and only remember the nasty one. I remember walking down the steps on to the set of *Aspel and Company* once, seeing a wall of friendly faces – except for one belonging to a lady sitting in the front row, arms crossed and a baleful expression on her face. It nearly threw me. I kept stealing glances in her direction – she soon lost the baleful expression – people look quite benign when they're asleep.

In newspapers I've been called bland and 'smoothy-chops' so often that it almost goes over my head now, and people go on about my baggy eyes as if I made them that way myself – which I suppose I did, in a way. But these days, if it looks as if it's going to be nasty, I take the easy way out. I don't read it.

It seems to me that it's better to be an actor as far as the critics are concerned. They might say you gave a good performance, or they may say you gave a bad one, but they rarely go into the realms of personal abuse. Sometimes you might even be lucky enough to be endowed with the qualities of the people you play – John Wayne, for example, was held up as being symbolic of everything that was good and right about America. Impressive though he undoubtedly was, if you analyse his career, all he did was put make up on his face and pretend to be somebody else.

At one time or another my guests have all suffered the slings and arrows of outrageous critics . . .

BARRY MANILOW Criticism hurts – what can I tell you? It hurts. But there's one part of me that says, 'I'm glad that I'm still popular enough to be killed in the Press. Because who are they gonna kill – some poor snook who's out of work, or the guy that's on top? So I'm glad that after ten years of making records, and ten years of being on the road, I'm still popular enough to get insulted by the Press. I just feel that it insults the fans even more than it does me. These days, I feel like it's embarrassing to say you're a Barry Manilow fan, but people still show up . . .

GLENDA JACKSON The ones you tend to remember are the worse ones, those that are particularly cruel. But there was one which I liked very much and which still makes me laugh, which wasn't to do with my performance, but with my appearance. It was 'The face that launched a thousand dredgers . . .' I think that's witty.

GEORGE MELLY Cilla Black won't speak to me to this day because when I was a critic, I wrote a very warm piece about her, but during the course of it, I said, 'She's quite good-looking, but she does have the nose of a rather careful boxer.' Apparently, she was so upset by this that she had a nose job.

MIKE YARWOOD A certain lady critic wrote, 'Mike Yarwood did a totally unrecognizable René from *'Allo 'Allo.'* Yes, it does hurt, especially when I've worked so damn hard trying to get it right. But the following day, I got a letter from Gorden Kaye, who plays the character, saying how much he enjoyed it. I thought, 'Well, if it's good enough for him, it's OK for me.'

MARGARET THATCHER All the cartoons are very funny – I think cartoonists are marvellous. Some of the other remarks, though – well, they hurt. I find it very difficult when you have a journalist round, and you will perhaps cooperate as much as you can with an interview, and then sometimes they'll go and dip their pen in acid and write really horrid things. I've learned to live with it, because if it looks horrid, or someone tells me it's horrid, I won't read it.

ALAN BATES I had a particularly gruesome review quite recently. I did a film called *Prayer For The Dying*. In London and America it had notices which ranged from very good to absolutely appalling. There was one which came to me from America which said, 'Alan Bates plays his part in a style which makes Bela Lugosi seem a master of nuance.' I rather love that one.

GARY WILMOT I don't collect criticisms, but the worst one I ever had was when they completely left me out of the write-up. That said everything for me.

ANJELICA HUSTON The reviews of my first film were not great. They called me wooden and unattractive. I still stutter when I say those words!

GRIFF RHYS JONES 'It's the sort of performance we would expect from an understudy,' was one review I had.

JUDI DENCH The first part I ever did at the Old Vic was Ophelia, in 1957. And the critic Richard Findlater, who later went on to become a dear friend, said, 'How dare the English equivalent of a national theatre employ a schoolgirl, whom none of us has heard of, and who can't do it?' And at the time I was desperately shocked by it, as you always are by bad notices – you always remember the bad ones and never the good. But later, I realized that it had been quite good for me and stopped me getting big-headed.

JOHN MILLS I remember one notice which said, 'John Mills walks across the stage looking like a bewildered carrot ...' A bewildered carrot! I thought it was fantastic!

SARAH BRIGHTMAN We had a première of *Requiem*, and one of the main critics had a real go at it – and at me – and I remember sitting up in bed with Andrew and just wanting to weep. It's quite a horrible thing when you've worked on something so hard, but you have to go through it. And there are times, like with *Phantom of the Opera*, where we got wonderful reviews, so we were laughing and happy.

TONY CURTIS Critics don't know nothing. Critics should not have jobs. They should not be paid £250 a week to write about movies that cost £50 million and then tell you how bad it is.

OUCH!

I remember asking John Lennon if those were his own teeth, and he answered, 'Yes. Are those your own spots?'

— Dusty Springfield

A good put-down, one that does away with your ego in one fell swoop, can be shattering. It can also be funny and it can do you a power of good. When I was a TV newscaster, I was enjoying my new-found fame, and signing some autographs up in Manchester, when an old lady said, 'Who's he?' 'He reads the news,' someone told her. 'Well, what do you want his bloody autograph for, just because he reads the bloody news?' she said. She was right, of course. I just wish she hadn't said it.

Another time I was lying in a hospital bed after a car crash – I'd been lucky and escaped with minor injuries, but I've always had a keen sense of drama, so I lay there feeling as though I'd just come through the Battle of Britain. I could hear two nurses talking in the corridor outside. 'Quiet,' said one. 'Michael Aspel's in there – the man who reads the news, he's smashed his car.' 'Oh dear,' gasped the other. 'Thank God it wasn't Robert Dougall.' Quite often the real 'you' doesn't live up to people's expectations of the 'television' version. Once, in a crowded bar I was forced into conversation with two ladies who were so disappointed that I felt quite guilty. 'Not as tall as you expected,' I said. 'No, not as good-looking, either,' they said. 'What a let-down.'

But at least they knew it was me. Some time ago I turned up at Broadcasting House to meet someone for lunch. I announced his name at Reception, and the girl rang up the guy and said, 'Your taxi's here ...' Not long after that blow to the ego, I turned up at a studio to do a commercial. I stood there with a suit on my shoulder and said who I was. The receptionist rang through and said, 'Michael Aspel's clothes have arrived.'

Perhaps the best one of all happened again at the good old reception desk at the BBC, but this time not to me. Apparently they were doing a programme about monarchs who'd lost their thrones and gone into exile. Quite a number of them were turning up at the BBC and the harassed receptionist was heard to say, as she reported the arrival of yet another, 'I'm sorry, where did you say you were king of?'

In my experience the smart rejoinder to a put down usually occurs to me on the bus on the way home, but at least some of my guests were quick thinking enough to exact their revenge ...

VINCENT PRICE The other day I was on a plane, and a man came up to me and was absolutely thrilled to see me. He said, 'Give me your autograph, Mr Karloff.' So I did – and I signed it Peter Lorre.

DENIS HEALEY One of my best-known remarks was when I was Chancellor and Geoffrey Howe was my opponent, and he made a rather damaging criticism of what I was doing and I didn't want to spend time on that. I thought it was better to put my *own* thing forward so I dismissed his comment by saying that his rude attack on me was like being savaged by a dead sheep – and that became famous. But when I became spokesman in opposition myself and he was the Foreign Secretary and we were sparring partners again, I made a nice remark about him and he said it was like being nuzzled by an old ram. So I got up immediately and said it would be the end of a beautiful friendship if he accused me of necrophilia! I think on the whole it pays to try to use humour, but it's better not to be too cruel if you can avoid it.

ROY CASTLE My grandad was a barber and my mother was a hairdresser so they taught me how to cut hair and it came in very useful, especially when I did National Service. There was one lad who was a real bully, and he says, 'Give me a hair cut.' So I said OK, and I gave him a real fancy one – it was like topiary, and I left him with a rude word on the back of his head.

PATRICK LICHFIELD I remember a man coming up to me at Sandhurst and looking at the back of my hair and saying, 'What regiment are you going into?' and I said 'The Grenadiers,' and he said 'You appear to be growing your own bear skin.' I love the story about King Hussein who was a cadet there. Apparently he was fidgeting on parade and the Sergeant Major screamed at him, 'Stand still, you idle little monarch!' It certainly puts you in your place.

DENIS NORDEN I love the story told to me by a make-up girl who used to work for a well-known London hairdresser. Seeking to flatter one of his customers one day, he said to her. 'Has anybody ever told you that you look like an older version of Jacqueline Bisset?' And of course it was her!

MICHAEL CAINE I was standing outside the Beverly Wilshire Hotel, in Los Angeles, talking to Cary Grant, when a woman saw me and she shrieked, 'You're him!' She said, 'I've been here for three weeks, I haven't seen one movie star until now,' and she came over and got my autograph. And then she turned to Cary Grant, and said, 'You never see any movie stars, do you?' And he said, 'No, my dear, you don't . . .'

PAMELA STEPHENSON I was once doing a live phone-in programme and this woman rang up and she said, 'I used to think that your impersonation of Princess Anne was needlessly cruel and unpleasant, but now I realize that they were, in fact, your own teeth.'

TONY CURTIS When I first started in movies, the magazines used to have competitions in which they'd say, 'Win Tony Curtis for a weekend . . .' with second and third prizes of a refrigerator and a washing machine and so on. Well, this woman in Washington won me, and I can tell you she was really pissed off. I had to spend the weekend with her and her family, but she was so disappointed – I could tell by her behaviour. So eventually I said, 'Look, is everything all right?' and she said, 'Oh, sorry, it's got nothing to do with you, it's just that I wanted the washing machine.'

JENNY AGUTTER After my early success in *The Railway Children*, I thought acting was the most wonderful thing. At 11 years old it was magical to be making films – you were treated like a star, and I was very proud of myself. And of course when you're playing a lead role, everybody's very careful that your make-up looks right and they come and powder your face and brush your hair before every shot. I was having all that done one day and I heard one little girl say to another, 'Why do they keep doing her make-up?' And I thought, 'Well, because I'm the star, of course.' But the other little girl had a better answer. 'Because she's so untidy,' she said.

Years later, I was doing a scene where I had to murder my husband – it was a very dramatic scene and it was in the pit at the Royal Shakespeare Company, so it was just this tiny little theatre, with everybody sitting very close to you, and you can see everybody, and you can hear everything. So I'm stabbing my husband and it all got quite wild and my hair started coming down. And I heard one woman in the audience say, 'Look, her hair pins have just fallen out.' And this is just after I've murdered my husband!

DAVID FROST I remember about six weeks into the first nationally televised programme I ever did, going into Harrods to buy something. I took out my cheque book, and the guy behind the counter said, 'Oh, Mr Frost, we never miss your show,' and I said, 'Oh, that's very nice,' and carried on writing. He said, 'You know, if my wife and I are out, we make sure we're back by 10.30 in the evening . . .' and I said, 'Oh, that's lovely, thank you.' And he went on: 'And if we're at home, we make sure we've eaten and washed up before the show.' So I said, 'How nice, thank you,' and handed him over the cheque. And he said, 'Do you have any means of identification?'

Now, I can't sing – I've never sung for anyone, I just can't do it. But I was promoting a Neil Diamond concert and one day he got me up on stage during this tour, and introduced me to the audience. Well that was OK, but then, to my horror, he got me to join in singing one of his songs. I desperately tried to do it, but I was pathetic. I'd told him before that I couldn't sing a note but he'd obviously ignored it. But after the concert, he said to me, 'You were quite right, you really can't sing.'

CHARLTON HESTON Charlton was my mother's maiden name – it's an English surname and I've been comfortable with it, but at the beginning it gave me one of the worst experiences of my childhood. I had just moved down to a new school from a small village near the Canadian border where I was raised, and on my first day at school, the teacher calls the roll. She got to my name and said, 'Er, Charlotte Heston? Charlotte? Where's the little Heston girl?'

JACKIE COLLINS Someone rang me up on a phone-in programme, and he said 'I read your book, I think it's absolutely disgusting.' And I said, 'Well, why did you read it, it's hardly a secret that I write about sex.' And he said, 'I asked the librarian if she had something with big print so she gave me your book.'

VICTORIA WOOD I've played in a certain town that makes linoleum where the audience did not laugh once. Not once. They went through the whole show in complete silence. And then just as I left the stage, sobbing, I heard somebody say, 'Well, I don't admire her dress-sense.'

PAUL McCARTNEY I was once rung up by the great Frank Sinatra himself. He said, 'I've heard about you, have you got a song for me?' Now, it's every song-writer's dream that Frank Sinatra will ask you for a song, and I had one all ready. 'I've got just the one, Frank,' I said. And then he turned it down.

TWIGGY I went to New York in the 60s and I had a funny experience with a man who was an unknown at the time, a new young comic called Woody Allen. He wasn't exactly nasty to me but I was only sixteen and I hadn't done many interviews, and I was nervous. We sat on our stools and I smiled at him, thinking he was going to ask me about my dress or where I lived or something, and he said, 'Who's your favourite philosopher?' Well, now I'd know what to do but then I just looked at him for help, and said, 'I don't know any.' And he said, 'Oh come on, you must have a favourite philosopher, everyone's got one.' So I said, 'I don't know any – who's *your* favourite philosopher?' And he said, 'Well, your Greeks and your Romans.' And I said, 'Yes, but what are their names?' 'You know,' he said, 'your Greeks and your Romans.' And at that point he made his chair tip over because he didn't know any either.

GRIFF RHYS JONES People usually remember Mel Smith because he looks like a potato. I was picked up by a taxi driver once and we were going along and he said, 'Oh, I know that voice – oh, don't tell me – you're Jeremy Pascal, aren't you?' And I said, 'No, I'm not Jeremy Pascal', so he said, 'You should try going on the radio, you sound just like him.' As we turned the corner Mel was ambling up out of an underground car park – he'd been parking his Rolls-Royce or something. The driver said, 'Look, there's Mel Smith over there, coming out of the car park,' and I said, 'Mel's supposed to be coming with me, we're supposed to be going to Television Centre.' So I opened the door and I shouted to Mel. But the driver said, 'Don't call him over, for heaven's sake!' But Mel got in the cab and the cabbie never said another word.

GARY WILMOT Once a guy came running after me, he must have run fifty yards up the road, but I had to ignore it, because I can't be big-headed enough to turn round and go, 'Oh, he's running after me.' So I kept walking. And he caught up with me, and went, 'Oi! You're – um – you're – er – you're – er – 'and I said 'Gary Wilmot?' And he went, 'Nah . . .,' and walked away!

Lenny Henry tells me how much he's enjoying the show!

Su Pollard and Michael Caine.

Deborah Kerr and Kirk Douglas, two of my all-time favourites.

FRIENDS, HEROES, COUNTRYMEN

I used to try and look like Elvis and sing like Little Richard.

— Paul McCartney

One of the best things about doing a talk show is that you get the chance to meet people you've admired for years. The danger is that they might turn out to be entirely different from how you expected them to be. They have every right to be different — it's very presumptious of us to invent personalities for them simply because we've seen them act on a cinema screen, but it can still be a shock when they're not as you'd hoped. Disappointments are rare and sometimes people are even better than you'd imagined. I've had a few of my heroes on the show — Elizabeth Taylor, Lauren Bacall, Deborah Kerr, and Daniel J. Travanti from *Hill Street Blues*, but I've still got a hit list. It's sad that so many of the people I'm interested in are no longer around. Three and four decades ago, I was a star-struck cinema-goer who could think of no better way to pass a morning, afternoon or evening than by visiting the local flea-pit. That's the thing about heroes — they tend to reflect the goings-on in your life, and that's why I'm always interested to know who others like.

A few times, the show has been the catalyst in bringing fans together. Joanna Lumley had always had a passion, as she put it, for Dirk Bogarde; Dustin Hoffman was a fan of Sting; John Lennon had been a great Monty Python fan, and so Yoko was delighted to meet John Cleese. They all met for the first time on the show. A lot of my guests will know each other already, and some, like George Harrison and Ringo Starr, are close friends. Others, like Stewart Granger, for example, will just come on and be wonderfully indiscreet. And when chat turns to gossip – well, that's another fine show I've gotten you into.

STEWART GRANGER I made a film in India called *Bhowani Junction*, with Ava Gardner. Ava was intrigued with me – she wasn't in love but she was intrigued – because I wouldn't go out with her as I was married. I was married to Jean Simmons then and I didn't believe in screwing around if you were married, which today is rather square, isn't it? But I wouldn't go out with Ava because she was very attractive, and I'm only human and it would only have taken a couple of drinks and then we'd have started something. But one night she broke into my bedroom at 2 o'clock in the morning. Well, it was very hot in India, and so I was sleeping naked, and I just went 'Ahhh ...' and pulled the sheets up. So Ava said, 'What's the matter with you, are you queer or something?' After that, she was always having a go at me and one day we were doing a love scene and suddenly she popped her tongue in my mouth. 'Ava!' I said. 'How dare you! What do you think you're doing? Don't ever do anything like that again ...' That's how square I was. ...

CLINT EASTWOOD I feel that people are disappointed if I don't look at them and say, 'Make my day,' or something like that. I remember being on a show much like this one, and Mohammad Ali, who was the champion at that time and who I'd never met, was there. He said to me, 'Come here, I want to talk to you,' and he took me down into the basement of the studio, through some hallway that had a lot of pipes running down it, around the corner, where nobody else was, and he said, 'I've got to talk to you. Will you give me that look that you give in those films and tell me I've got ten minutes to get out of town?' But of course he was the heavyweight champ so I told him that I didn't have a gun with me and didn't do it.

TONY CURTIS Marilyn Monroe was difficult. She was a pain in the ass and difficult to work with and when we were making *Some Like It Hot*, Jack Lemmon and I had to get dressed up as women. We'd get in there at six in the morning and by 9.30 we were ready to shoot, complete with wig, make-up and women's dresses. We'd have to sit around like that for four or five hours waiting for Marilyn to show up. Now, the poor woman was suffering and that was a problem for her but still, we had to sit around all day long. And Billy Wilder said to us, 'Now listen, guys, you'd better get your lines right every time because the first time she gets it right, I'm going to print it.' That meant the pressure on Jack and me was incredible, and I just thought it was unfair – after all, we were all making a living. There's no question about Marilyn's genius, her ability to do what she did. No question. Yet by the same token, as a person, she was disagreeable.

BOB NEWHART The one picture I did with Steve McQueen was called *Hell is for Heroes*. It was the first movie I ever made and I'd never expected to make a motion picture at all, so it all took me aback rather. Steve was a method actor and his character wasn't supposed to like us. He came up and said to us: 'Would you mind if I don't talk to you, because I'm not supposed to like you in the movie, and I'm afraid I'll get to know you?' So we said fine, and he didn't talk to us for the whole length of the movie.

DEBORAH KERR When I arrived at MGM, I felt like I was going back to an enormous boarding school again. I didn't see the same face twice for three weeks – there were so many sound stages and all these people, and on top of that, I was going to make a movie with Clark Gable. Well, I sat in that room and saw this fantastic-looking man come through the door and I just didn't believe it. Never in my wildest dreams had I ever thought I would even go to Hollywood, let alone work with people like him.

TOM HANKS The greatest star I ever met was Bette Davis. It was at the Academy Awards and they assign you seats, and I was there with my lovely girlfriend (now my wife), and we went off to dance. When we came back, Bette Davis was sitting in my girlfriend's seat. 'Honey,' I said, 'Bette Davis is in your seat.' Someone else at our table said, 'Oh, kick her out, she'll love it, honestly, I know she'll love it.' So I went over to Miss Davis and I said, 'Excuse me, Miss Davis, you are sitting in my girlfriend's seat, but if anybody can, you can.' Bette Davis said, 'HUH?' So I said, 'Well, er, Miss Davis, you're sitting in my girlfriend's seat, but if anybody can, you can.' And Bette Davis turned to me and said, 'I can't hear a word you're saying . . .' That was the biggest thrill of my life!

TELLY SAVALAS I was with the State Department in the information services, assigned to the United Nations. I met all kinds of glorious people – President Eisenhower (General, at the time); your own Sir Winston Churchill – great guy; and Eleanor Roosevelt, too. It's a strange thing but I wasn't at all nervous with these people. Then I became an actor and I went to Hollywood, and had stars in my eyes and I made a picture with Burt Lancaster. I promise you, although I wasn't nervous in front of Winston Churchill, I couldn't catch my breath with Burt Lancaster. So you see how the screen blows everything out of proportion.

TWIGGY When I went to Los Angeles, the people at MGM film studios said to me, 'Do you want to meet anyone famous?' 'Oh yes,' I said, 'I'd love to meet Fred Astaire.' And they said, 'That's a bit tricky because he's very private and doesn't go out ...' So I said, 'Fine, I wouldn't infringe on his privacy but you asked me, and that's who I'd like to meet.' Well, while we were having this conversation, there was a lady in the office who used to work for Fred Astaire and when I left she rang him up. And she called me later, and said, 'Excuse me, but I just talked to Fred and I told him the story, and he's invited you to tea tomorrow at his house.' It was the dream of my life, it was great.

So we went up, and we got to know him, and he was absolutely gorgeous, of course. The next time I went to Los Angeles, I called him and we took him out to dinner. We took him to a Chinese restaurant where they serve those drinks in coconuts – they're quite strong and he doesn't really drink, but we made him have one anyway, and he quite enjoyed it. And by the time we came out we were all a little bit tiddly, and as you know, Fred doesn't dance any more, but as we walked up the street to the car, he started to tap dance. I couldn't believe it! He did a double pirouette, landed on his knees and said, 'Hollywood – I love you.' It was great, and all those people driving past, saying, 'You know, I think that was Fred Astaire dancing ...'

ROBBIE COLTRANE I went to see *The Wild One* many many years ago when I was thinking about becoming an actor and thinking maybe it was a bit of a poofy thing to do, and Marlon Brando was standing in front of this juke box and he had 'New York Rebels' on the back of his leather jacket and this girl came up and said, 'What are you rebelling against, Johnny?' and he says 'What have you got?' and I thought, 'Yeah, that's my man, I'll do that.'

CLIFF RICHARD It was Elvis who kindled my interest in music. The people who were on the radio when I first got into listening were really fine singers, people like Perry Como, Frank Sinatra and Bing Crosby, but good as they were, they didn't inspire me to be like them. But when I heard Elvis, I couldn't, I really couldn't, believe the noise that came out of him. The awful thing is that I had a chance to meet him. In 1976 I went to the States to promote 'Devil Woman' and some journalist said to me, 'If you'd like to meet Elvis, I can arrange it.' But Elvis was going through a very fat period, and I thought, 'Well, I'll wait until he's lost some weight,' because my childhood image was of a real animal of a person. And then of course he upped and died, far too early in life. I always wish now that I'd met him.

DENNIS WATERMAN I'm afraid George Cole came off worst from our partnership in *Minder*. He taught me a great deal about *The Times* crossword, and I taught him how to swear.

DUSTIN HOFFMAN I was renting a house with my family on the beach in Malibu and I'd just had my birthday – it was August 8th – and they gave me a rubber dinghy. I went out in it with my wife, who was eight months pregnant, and when we got back I couldn't pull it ashore and I wouldn't let my wife help because she was pregnant. And I was just looking around, struggling, and I heard this guy with a strange way of talking. He was sitting on a dune with about a week's growth of beard and a wet suit pulled down to his waist, just sitting there like a bum, saying 'Can I help you with that?' And I said, 'Oh yes, thanks,' and he came over and with one hand just took the dinghy out, and I went back into the house with my wife. I said, 'Boy, he's really strong. I think that's an English accent – I think he's in the rock business.' She said, 'Don't you know who that was?' And I said, 'No.' She said, 'That was Sting.' And of course I called up my daughter and told her. I felt very bad about it. The next day I was out fishing on my dinghy and there was Sting windsurfing, and we never spoke to each other.... I didn't know what to say to him.

GEORGE HARRISON I believe that there was never a time when you didn't exist and will never be a time when you cease to exist. The only thing that changes is our bodily condition, soul comes into the body and we go from birth to death, and how I look at it is that death is like taking your suit off. The soul is in these three bodies and one body falls off. And like that I can feel John around here . . .

HIGH SOCIETY

I know you can't say armpit in front of Royalty.

— Victoria Wood

The Queen would be a marvellous guest to have on *Aspel and Company* – she has humour and a great sense of fun, and if it were possible to cut through all the protocol I'd sign her up on the spot.

I first met her – if 'met' is the right word – in 1968. I'd just come off the air after reading the news when I got a message to ring Brigadier Hardy Roberts, at Windsor Castle. My first thought – and it would have been yours, too, if you'd known the practical jokers I was working with – was that it was a giant send-up. But of course I made the phone call and was greeted by a crisp voice saying, 'Good evening. How kind of you to ring back. I'm Master of the Queen's Household and I'm instructed to invite you to lunch at Buckingham Palace with Her Majesty and Prince Philip on 17th May.' A week later, an invitation arrived confirming all that he'd said and if this was a practical joke, it was turning into the most elaborate one ever staged. Even when I arrived at the gates of Buckingham Palace, I half expected to be turned away.

'Would you care to park over here?' said a young army officer. I got out of the car and carefully locked the door. 'I think you'll find it still here when you come out,' he said.

I was shown into the Bow Room and introduced to the other guests and a little while later, three corgies trotted into the room, followed by the Queen and Prince Philip. Introductions over, our conversation began. The day before, the Queen had opened the mammal house at London Zoo, where day is turned into night so that visitors can watch nocturnal animals. 'What did you think of it, Ma'am?' I ventured. 'I should think it would be the perfect place for an assignation,' she said. Shortly afterwards a helicopter landed in the grounds. 'I do wish they wouldn't do that,' said the Queen. 'It makes the windows so dusty.'

Since then I've met most of the Royal Family at various charity functions, although I don't quite have the full set. I have yet to curtsey before Prince Andrew, although I did interview his Spitting Image, and Fergie's too, on *Aspel and Company*, just after it was announced that Fergie was pregnant. And I'd love to meet the Queen Mother ... although I once had a gracious smile and a nod across a crowded foyer, so I could almost claim that one.

I was once standing next to an actor who was having a wonderful conversation with Princess Anne. They had a complete misunderstanding – she was talking about the Royal Tournament and he thought she was talking about *Dallas*. Everyone who could hear it was just weeping with laughter, and in the end she just said, 'Hmmm, the mind boggles ...' and wandered off.

Politicians don't have quite the same effect, I know, but I think that as the dividing line seems to be getting ever more blurred, they can share this chapter.

DAME EDNA EVERAGE I get a lot of calls from the members of the Royal Family, as a matter of fact. You know this chat line that was closed down by British Telecom? Well, it was mainly because the Queen and I were using it night and day. We were.

Fergie (have you heard of her?) and her husband, the Duke and Duchess of York, they've got this little baby and they wanted to call it Edna, after me – as a little tribute. But I said it would give it too much to live up to. You know, a lot of people criticized Fergie because she went all the way to Australia and didn't take the kiddie with her. I advised her to do that. I said, 'Look, they've got enough babies in Australia.' I said, 'It's dangerous taking kiddies to Australia – they may get molested by marsupials on the apron of the airport.' So I looked after little Bea.

Yes, I babysat the Royal baby. In fact, as soon as I held this little baby in my arms, I ruined my Giorgio Armani blouse. As a matter of fact, looking at you now, a lot of my maternal instincts are surging – I'm glad I'm wearing my nursing pads.

TOM JONES When I was doing the Royal Knockout show, I said to Princess Anne, 'We're going to have to have a rallying song, but what kind of song should we sing?' She said, 'We don't have to have a song, we just have to win.'

WAYNE SLEEP I was doing this charity gala and Prince Philip was in the box and unfortunately, my partner, Cherry Gillespie, was looking at me with rather a frown on her face, and I thought, 'There's something wrong' but I didn't know what it was. When I eventually managed to look down, I realized that my flies were completely undone and not only that, the button had come away from the top ... I apologized to Prince Philip afterwards. He said, 'Oh no, not at all my boy, it's perfectly all right. The same thing happened to me.' I said, 'Well, how did you know?' And he said, 'I was playing polo and I suddenly felt a breeze.'

The Princess of Wales loves dancing, as you know, she always wanted to be a dancer. I knew she did dance classes and she used to come and watch me from the wings when I was doing the musical *Dash*. She used to sit in the wings because, if she was out front, it had to be official and everybody would look to see her reaction and they wouldn't look at me, so I wasn't having that! But anyway, she used to come and watch and she said that it would be lovely to do a dance together one day. The problem was we were always in different parts of the world, but in the end we managed to get together and do a little number. I was far more nervous than she was – she knew the routine, I didn't. I choreographed it but as soon as I'd done it, I went to do a pantomime somewhere. But she worked on it and she got it right.

LULU I'm not one of those people who's easily impressed, but I'll tell you, last year I was driving up Sloane Street in London and there's a car coming down the other side. And I looked, and looked again, and sure enough, it was Princess Diana. So I got home and I said to my mother, 'Ma, you'll not believe it, I'm driving up Sloane Street, you know who's coming the other way?' I said, 'Princess Diana.' I was so excited. Mum said, 'Did she see you?' I said, 'Mother, she doesn't know who I am!' But funnily enough, the next night, I had to go to a charity do and Princess Diana was there and I was introduced to her. I was standing in line, really dying to get a good look at her and say hello to her, because I think she's fabulous, and she came up, and the first thing she said was, 'I saw you yesterday driving up Sloane Street, but I didn't wave because I didn't think you'd know who I was.' She really did say that! And that really impressed me, you can imagine.

MICHAEL CAINE I think Prince Andrew does a great job. He just did one soppy thing when he squirted paint over the Press. But I was so upset when I read a lot of the British papers. I thought, 'Jesus, this guy has knocked himself out here – he's made one really soppy mistake, OK?' But that was the only thing they printed about him. It was quite incredible. I read a paper the day before yesterday and it said, ' . . . his so-far useless existence,' and I thought to myself, 'Does that mean that everybody who fought in the Falklands has had a so-far useless existence?' Here is a young man to whom we've said, 'You've got to go out and be like everybody else, you've got to go up to the front and be in the firing line' and this guy did it. And they say, 'Be a real sailor.' And then when he comes home on leave and acts like a real sailor, they say, 'Oh, no, we want a prince.'

I had dinner once with the Queen and I was sitting one away from her and of course you don't address her unless she talks to you first, but anyway, the man next to her obviously wasn't too scintillating and she finally leaned across him, and said, 'Mr Caine.' I said, 'Yes, Ma'am?' She said, 'Do you know any jokes?' So I said, 'Yes, I do, do you know any?' She said, 'Yes,' and we started to tell jokes. I'd always had an image of her, usually at some boring event or other, where she sits and looks kind of cold. I'd never met her before, but I thought she was very warm, very charming. I was quite taken with her.

GERMAINE GREER I don't see why Fergie should take a bashing about her clothes. I mean, we've got one clothes horse. And she is a funny girl, I love the way she speaks. She has a lovely voice and she always expresses herself nicely. I mean, she's never really going to look terrific, is she now, let's face it. Some of us just can't make it.

Before a Royal visit, the Australians all talk republican: 'The problem with this country is that we took too much from the Brits, we got the class system, the old school tie and all that,' they'll say. But all you have to get is one smile from Princess Di, one suggestion that she is actually enjoying herself and everyone says, 'Oh, isn't it nice!' In fact, there is a school of thought that says the Queen is going to emigrate because the British are getting so stroppy. She'd probably have a better time down there.

BOB GELDOF I thought President Mitterand was good fun. He told me a good story about when he got to be the President of France. Apparently he got handed all these things with 'Top Secret' on them and he thought, 'This is the business.' He was having a cabinet meeting one day, when he got an envelope with 'Top Secret For The President's Eyes Only' written on it. He opened it up, and there was another envelope inside. He opened that, and eventually, like a Russian doll, got to the real envelope and he opened that – and it was the menu for lunch that day.

I'm not a friend of Prince Charles, but we've met a couple of times and I like him as a man, and he's very bright and also very charming. And I think quite brave.

Prince William wasn't so charming. He was a three-year-old, which I was quite used to, having one myself, so I knew how to deal with him and told him to shut up.

MIKE YARWOOD When Margaret Thatcher became Prime Minister, I decided that I wasn't going to impersonate her because she was a lady and it would be best left to ladies to do, but I thought, 'Well, I do need *something* – I need somebody, a VIP impersonation,' and that was when I decided to become 'royal'. Some time later, I went to a charity function and had dinner with Prince Charles. We were at a table for ten people, but my wife and myself were fortunate enough to sit next to him. In fact, she spoke to him more than I did because she was actually sitting right next to him and he said, 'Does he practise at home, Mrs Yarwood?' So she said, 'Oh yes, he does. He spends a lot of time on each of his characters.' She said, 'In fact, I actually lived with you for two weeks.' And Prince Charles said, 'If only I'd known, if only I'd known. . . .'

I met Neil Kinnock soon after he became the new leader of the Labour Party and then I met him again when I'd just done my first ever impression of him, complete with ginger wig, and I said, 'What did you think?' And he said, 'Well, I thought it was very good, really, but you seem to have too much hair.' And he wanted to borrow the wig so he could wear it himself.

Harold Wilson had a particular fascination for me. He was my hit record really, like a singer has a hit record. He became part of me. In fact, the first time I ever met him, I felt that we knew each other very well.

Over the years, I've met a lot of the Royal Family. I think possibly though, the most exciting moment was meeting the Queen because she's the monarch. I've met her on five or six occasions. . . . On the last Royal Show I did, I'd done Prince Charles in my act, and she said, 'How long have you been doing this?' And I said, 'Well, actually, I've been doing it quite some time now.' Then I started to gesticulate like Prince Charles, and she said, 'Mmm, yes, that is very nice.' But just as she was going, she said, 'You really *must* stop doing that with your hands.' It was very curt, the way she put it.

JANET BROWN Mrs Thatcher's very good about my impressions of her, although I was a little bit unnerved the very first time I met her at the House of Commons, because I went in there and I thought, 'She'll talk about the impersonation,' but she didn't mention it at all – and that made me feel even more nervous.

NORMAN TEBBIT I remember one occasion (I'll probably be put in jail for this because I think it's a Cabinet secret) when we were having a discussion and the Prime Minister said, 'That's all very well, we're talking about it from our point of view, but what do normal people think about this?' Then she turned round to George Younger and said, 'George, you're normal, what do you think?' And with this everybody burst out laughing and there was this pause before she said, 'Oh, men . . .'

PATRICK LICHFIELD I've got a little sea-horse tattooed on my arm. It's an embarrassment now, but I had it done the day I left the army, which was October 14, 1962 – you know, you never forget that day. Shortly afterwards, I was sent off to do a rather important photographic assignment in Denmark, photographing the then King of Denmark's youngest daughter. I arrived at the Palace, and the page showed me into a room and said, 'You'll have to wait because nobody is here.' After about two hours I got more and more finger-nail biting and worried. Eventually he came in again and said, 'The Queen is waiting and having tea with everybody else, would you like to go in?' Now, in those days, I must explain, I didn't have any money, I just had one rather odd suit and not much else but I put it all on as best I could. I got into the room, and the Queen got up and she poured the tea out, right to the very top of the cup, and with all the time in the world she passed it over towards me. I was simply shaking like a jelly. And as I put my hand out, the King noticed that I was nervous and said, 'Take your jacket off,' and he took his off. But as I took my jacket off, the most awful truth dawned on me – I hadn't got a sleeve. I had a cuff and cuff-links but nothing from my wrist up. But then he saw this tattoo on my arm and he looked at it and said, 'That was done by Mr Bradshaw in the Waterloo Road wasn't it?' and I said, 'How do you know?' and he said, 'I've got one, too.' And he took his trousers off . . . He had lots and lots and lots.

TRAVELLERS' TALES

I don't get along with air stewardesses. I'm sorry, but they are very bitchy. I ask them, 'Where is my seat?' They tell me, 'Three inches below where it was last year.'

— Joan Rivers

The first time I ever left England, I was eighteen years old and doing my National Service. We went to Germany and it was one of the most significant events of my life. I'd been away from home before – four-and-a-half years as an evacuee, followed by a term at a school in Hampshire – but I'd always suffered badly from homesickness. The excitement of seeing another country seemed to cure me of that, and happily, I never suffered those miserable pangs again.

I might have been a late starter but I made up for lost time. For a while I was never happier than when packing a suitcase, just about to set off for a new destination. I've been to most places that I'm interested in, with the exception of Russia, which was the one that got away. It happened when I was reading the news, and the plan was that we should have an exchange of film crews – the Russians would go to Bournemouth, and we would go to Yalta. Unfortunately, the trip coincided with the Six-Day War, and as our producer was Jewish, and the Russians were on the side of the other lot, we never did make it to the USSR.

These days I'm most attached to Italy – the climate, the food, the language, the people. We get over there whenever we can. But even when you travel, you don't really get away. I've often been standing looking at the sights when someone has come up and said, 'Hello, Mike – how's the show going?' Or 'Blimey, Aspel, what are doing here?' as if I'd crept out of the box without permission.

I was very pleased to learn that *Aspel & Company* is being seen in, among other places, Australia. My parents lived there several decades ago, and in more recent years, two of my sons. I've only been there three times, on family matters, but I liked what I saw. The last time I was in Melbourne, I decided to walk from my hotel to my son's place, a distance the hotel staff thought was suicidal for an out-of-condition middle-aged Pom. In my ultra-casual sportswear, I managed the distance, but got lost half-way. I stopped a young woman to ask directions. She took several paces back and gasped, 'Michael Aspel!' Blimey, I thought, the show must have really registered out here. She turned out to be an English teacher who'd only arrived in Australia the day before. The shock at seeing someone she would have expected to be adorning some distant television studio in a natty suit was almost too much for her. Australia seems to have become the Mecca for Entertainers. Most of them love the place.

Most people come back from their travels with tales of adventure along with their sun-tans and duty-frees. A different language, different cultures and customs and the undeniable hassle that accompanies some journeys may make you wish you had stayed at home at the time, but the anecdotes keep everyone amused for years afterwards.

Funny things happen to the famous too, on their way to places. . . .

VICTORIA WOOD I once had to fly from Aberdeen to Newcastle because it was the only way we could get there in time and I was with a girl who'd never been on a shuttle flight before and I was saying, 'Well, it won't be a very big plane and there'll only be one air hostess and it will be the one with the swollen ankles and the lipstick on her teeth, you know, it's not going to be very high class.' Then we saw this tiny thing like something out of a cereal packet and that was our plane and we had to get on it, and I thought 'The only way this is going to get up – it was like a Renault 5 with wings – the only way it's going to get off the ground is if somebody flaps their arms.' And they said to me, 'You've got short legs, you can sit down the front.' So I went down the front and I said, 'Are you sure, because there's a steering wheel and a gear lever here.' And they said, 'Yes, you go where the co-pilot goes,' and then this man came on in a pullover with crumbs all down it and he was the pilot – I thought, 'A pilot is

Lauren Bacall.

Zsa Zsa Gabor introduces
husband number 8 (9? 10?).

Joan Collins.

Well hello, Dolly.

Jodie Foster.

Su Pollard re-enacts a scene from Sweeney Todd.

My knuckles go white as Helen Mirren recalls her first nude scene.

supposed to have chiselled features and a raincoat' – and he sat down, and you know they normally say, 'This is Captain So-and-So, we'll be flying at so-and-so feet and these are the exits' – he just went, 'This is the door and soon as I've had me coffee we'll be off,' and he got out this thermos. And I thought, 'If he has a heart attack I'm going to have to fly this plane single-handed to Newcastle.' I was glued to his every move. I was watching all the little dials and he's pulling this in and pulling that out and I thought, 'No, I can't even work the cooker and the grill at the same time, so no chance.'

ALAN WHICKER I think travel's exciting, so when I'm going on a flight, I want to enjoy it. I can't be blasé about it even now, and I've been travelling all my life. To fly to Australia is a sensational thing to do, isn't it? The idea of going on board, as sensible people do, drinking Perrier water and not eating, taking pills, knocking themselves out and going zonk – you miss twenty-three very exciting hours that way. You have to relish these things, so I do everything wrong. I drink the champagne, eat the food, talk to the Captain – you know, just mingle and enjoy it. But of course I'm with the BBC and you know how generous they are. They'd like me to travel strap-hanging at the back but I won't do that. I upgrade myself, and I pay for myself because in *Whicker's World*, for example, we hit the ground and start filming. On the Australian series we arrived in mid-morning, having flown for twenty-three hours, gone through about six time zones and feeling slightly ga-ga. By that same evening, we were filming the Sleaze Ball in Sydney, which was attended by 6,000 homosexuals, half of whom seemed to be dressed up as 6-foot 6-inch nuns with beards. And in that sort of situation, you have to keep your wits about you.

I remember having a terrible flight in a little Iranian aircraft. The plane was bouncing around and the pilot got lost. At one point he turned around and said, 'Have you got a map?' It didn't do wonders for my confidence.

JOAN COLLINS In the past month, I haven't been longer than five days in one place without being on a plane – I was in London, then I went to Acapulco, I went to Los Angeles, and then Barbados, and then Miami, then Los Angeles again, and then I went to New York – I travel a lot. The pilot came up to me on the plane when we arrived about five hours ago, and he said, 'I want to know your secret. How do you do this – don't you suffer from jet-lag?' And when I said no, he said, 'Well, what do you do – I must try it.' I said, 'I sleep on the plane,' and he smiled and said, 'I don't think I can do that . . .'

FRANK CARSON A lot of people are frightened in aeroplanes. I was on one flying over from Dublin to here – it was Aer Lingus – it's actually known as Aer Fungus – and the plane was so old they found Lindbergh's lunch box.

MARGARET THATCHER In about 1967 I was going on my first tour to America – a speaking tour of about six weeks. I got everything ready, and everything I wanted was beautifully packed. In those days there was a big air station at Victoria, and you caught a bus from there. I handed over my ticket and passport, and the man said, 'Your passport is out of date.' Fortunately, it's my habit always to arrive early and I had got there an hour and a half before the bus left, so I simply called a taxi, dashed down to Petty France, got a renewal of my passport, got back got on the bus and caught the aircraft. But Denis is very different – he doesn't even get the day right. When we were first married he always travelled the world to try to get orders to keep the factory going. He went off on a six-week tour every year and that was the time when I knew I could get things done in the house. I always went to see him off, and on one occasion we turned up at that self-same air station, he handed over his ticket and the girl said, 'Your aircraft went this time yesterday.' But he wasn't in the least bit flustered. He said, 'Well, you'd better get me on the next one, then.'

GEORGE MELLY Airlines always choose the sort of film I would cross the road to avoid – long dramas about dying horses.

CLIVE JAMES I have this knack of falling asleep at will, like Ronald Reagan. Of course unlike him I have the knack of waking up again. But I don't really need a lot of sleep – eight hours' a day is enough, and twelve at night. I sleep easily on aircraft, for example – I can sleep right through a Roger Moore movie. But the chief hazard of flying on the intercontinental jets is too many Elliott Gould movies. I cannot stand movies with Elliott Gould in them. I once flew the world and saw three Elliott Gould movies on the way. When I landed I was just wrung out.

DAVE ALLEN I used to be a good traveller but I'm beginning to hate it now. I don't like airports to start with, because there are certain things which I find very uncomfortable. For example, you sit down on the seats and after about two minutes, you start to slide off them. So you get up and walk around, and you buy a paper you don't want, and you buy a coffee you don't want, and then you buy a drink to get rid of the coffee taste, and then you get pissed and they won't let you on the plane. I mean, even the Pope kisses the ground when he arrives anywhere – 'Thank God it's finished.'

KELLY MONTEITH I've worked a lot of ships – in fact, I worked the *QE2* and back, that was really an experience. People drink a lot on ships – an awful lot. And the reason they do that's because there's not much else to do, basically. First couple of days it's great because you walk up on deck, you say, 'Hey there's the ocean, look at that out there, it's so big ...' and then the second day you walk up and down and think, 'Boy, look at that ocean today, ain't that beautiful.' But after four, five days of that people walk up on deck, 'There's the Goddamn ocean again – stinking birds – to hell with it, let's go get a drink ...' And eat! After breakfast you walk on deck, there's a little snack and then you go sit by the pool and some guy brings you a sandwich. Then it's lunch, 'Oh, okay fine.' After lunch there is mid-afternoon buffet – you think, 'Gee, we just ate but, oh, what the hell, we're on holiday.' So you fill your plate up and eat that, and then they take that away, put out hors d'oeuvres, you nibble on those, and you go back to your cabin and change your clothes, because it's time for dinner. But it doesn't stop there – after dinner, you walk in, they're serving pizza, then after pizza – 'What's that ... midnight snack? Oh God!' You stop at the bar for a night-cap, and they're serving finger sandwiches. 'I've got to get away from this food – I'm going to bed.' You go back to your cabin, you open the door and there is a basket of fruit in your cabin. This whole damn ship is eatable. You know, a lot of people get on as passangers and get off as cargo.

FROM RUSSIA WITH LOVE...

DAVID STEEL I went on a student trip to the Soviet Union in the early 1960s. A group of us went out late at night in Moscow, and we were on the bus back home, when one of the students sitting next to me was sick down the back of a Russian soldier. I said, 'This is our stop!' He said, 'This *isn't* our stop,' but I said, 'It is now.' I had visions of Siberia, so I got him off ... he later became a Member of Parliament.

OMAR SHARIF I spent an awful twenty-seven weeks in Russia making what they call a mini series – an eight-hour production of *Peter the Great* – it was the worst experience of my whole life. For a start, it was very cold – it was the coldest winter in the last twenty or thirty years. Also, the food was terrible. I'd go to the restaurant at night and they had these menus in Russian and English. I told the waitress what I wanted in English and she'd look at the Russian translation and say, 'Niet.' There was just nothing there – I don't know if you know this word 'niet' – it is the most final thing you've ever heard. It's not like 'no' ... I mean, when somebody says 'no' to you, you can say, 'Well now, let's talk about this ...' 'Niet' is final.

Also, they have these very fat ladies who sit in all the corridors of the hotel. Every time you turn a corner there's another one, and you're not allowed any visitors in your room at all, so I got hold of an interpreter and I went to this lady, and I said, 'Tell this lady that I'm here for six months with no sex life at all.' And she said, 'Niet.' When I got back from there, I had to go to a health farm for a month, because I was not well at all. For the first time in my life I had high blood pressure!

KENNY EVERETT If you're single in Russia you get seven metres to live in – every flat is built to a certain size. I said to one woman there, 'Are you going to get married and have lots of children?' And she said, 'I must get married and have lots of children. For every child, you get a bigger flat – two more square metres.' So all they do in Russia is hump like mad so they can get bigger flats.

SEBASTIAN COE In Russia we had a KGB guy who was with us as a sort of team interpreter and general helper around the place, and one evening, a team official asked him where the nearest night club was. He looked over the top of his half-rimmed glasses and said, 'Helsinki.'

There was a general paranoia about the rooms. One of the BBC guys was absolutely sure that there was a bug in the room, and he systematically took the room to pieces. They went under the carpet, they pulled down light fittings, they did everything. They looked at the television in the corner and within seconds, the back was off and the entire contents of this television were spread out on the top of this table. And just as they were realizing that there was nothing there and putting it back, the phone went and a Russian voice at the other end said, 'Would you stop fiddling with your television set, please ...'

One of the press guys had a funny experience, too. He found what he thought was a little bug, a little nut actually underneath the carpet in the middle of the floor. He studiously started undoing it and there was a hell of a crash below ... it was the chandelier in the room below.

GEORGE COLE When you go anywhere abroad, you're always going to have people on the unit who hate the place before they get there. And we had several of those when we went to Russia. One of them said to me, 'Look, it's nothing to worry about, but watch out for the KGB detector vans.' I said, 'Oh, how do you know them?' He said, 'You can't miss them. They've got two big brass circular aerials on the top.' Well, I went out walking and suddenly saw a KGB detector van and I thought, 'What the hell are they detecting?' I mean, everybody knows what they are. So I asked one of the Russian actors. I said, 'These KGB detector vans, what is it they're after?' He fell on the floor laughing, and said, 'That's the car you hire when you get married, and those are wedding rings on the top.'

DENIS HEALEY I had an extraordinary experience when I was in Moscow celebrating the fortieth anniversary of D Day (representing Mrs Thatcher without her consent); I got separated from the other foreign guests because I wanted to help the ambassador to lay the official wreath, which was almost as large as a single poppy. And then I had to get into the Kremlin to the big meeting when Gorbachev was going to address everyone and the first woman astronaut and so on. And they wouldn't let me in. There was a young soldier standing at the gate of the Kremlin and I said, 'Delegatsia' –

you know. In desperation, I pulled out my wallet and showed him my old person's GLC bus pass and they let me through without any hesitation.

WAY DOWN UNDER

ALAN WHICKER There's a little island between Australia and New Zealand called Norfolk Island. It's only three miles by five and it's where *The Bounty* mutineers went to. It's my passion – I always say it's a little piece of Switzerland floating in the South Pacific, where nothing bites and nothing stings and they feed the pigs on wild peaches. It's a place of such joy, but it takes hours to get there from anywhere. Now it's populated mainly by viewers of *Whicker's World* who took one look and said, 'Right, that's for me,' and out they went.

MEL SMITH Understanding Australians can be a bit of a problem. They have very strange words for things. I mean, a stubby holder – do you know what a stubby holder is? I thought it was a pair of underpants. I really did. But it's the little canister that holds a short bottle of beer. They shorten everything, so it's barbie instead of barbecue and yachtie instead of yachtsman.

In Brisbane you have to be pretty law-abiding. In fact, while we were there they actually came up with a new law in Queensland which said that no bar could serve any sexual deviant, or homosexual. And people said, 'Well, how do we know if people are sexual deviants or homosexuals?' And the government said, 'You ask them.' So, it's rather odd, you walk in and you say, 'Can I have a beer?' And the barman says, 'Are you a child molester?' And you say, 'Yes' and he says, 'I'm sorry!' Very bizarre idea.

THE ENGLISHMAN AT HOME AND ABROAD...

VICTORIA WOOD I stay at huge hotels full of awful businessmen and there are always conferences – you walk in and there's always big notices up saying 'We are facing the future, we are going for it' and there's all these men in terrible creased suits – there's a crease running along the back where they've been sitting down having lectures and they don't know they're creased because men never look at their own backs and they never look at other men's backs in case people think they're gay. And they're all reeking of aftershave – Lynx and Cougar – there's a terrible whiff when you go in, and they come up to you and they've got these badges on saying, 'Hi, I'm Barry – I'm Going For It.' You go about saying, 'Hi, I'm Victoria – I'm knackered. I'm going to bed – please leave me alone.'

The worst thing about the lift is not only is it full of businessmen and aftershave – I have a theory that if enough businessmen with enough aftershave go into a lift the carpet will change colour like litmus paper – the worst thing about lifts is that they've always got pictures of bacon on the walls, which if you're a vegetarian and it's late at night is quite upsetting. I think my idea of purgatory is that I'll be in a lift with a lot of businessmen, with pictures of bacon on the walls, and there'll be music playing like Mozart, classical music like *The Moonlight Sonata* done on the bongos or something, and eventually, after purgatory has finished, we'll go down to the basement and the door will open and a man in a creased suit smelling of aftershave will come up saying, 'Hi, I'm the devil – I'm going for it.'

PATRICK MOORE I remember being in Japan once, and staying at a little hotel in the volcanic area – about two inches above Tokyo on the map. The first thing you do on going into a Japanese hotel is to take off your shoes. Well, my Japanese hosts took off their shoes, of course, but when I took off mine, I was acutely aware of a large hole in my sock, about which I could do nothing. In the end, I did the only thing I could think of, which was to carefully ink over that part of my foot! Also, when you go down to dinner in a Japanese hotel, you take off your European clothes and put on Japanese robes. They're very polite people but even they couldn't quite take me in a kimono and when I swept out of the dining-room, they were all doing their level best not to laugh. Finally I laughed first and then of course everybody just roared ...

STING I flew from Brazil to the Chingu River and you can't go there as a tourist because these Indians are very hostile, they have blow-pipes and rifles, and spears. But they showed me round the village and told me about their life and I have to say that it's the closest thing to paradise I've ever seen – they live in complete balance with their environment . . . it's very beautiful. And they did a fertility dance for me, and after that, they said, 'You're a singer, we want you to sing for us.' And there was a war party of chiefs sitting in a long line with rifles and machine guns. One of my songs is translated into Portuguese – they understand basic Portuguese – so I said, 'Normally I have lights and a PA,' and they went, 'What's that?' The percussionist who was with me went to a hut and borrowed some pots and he played on these pots and I sang unaccompanied apart from that. The Indians sat there with their fingers itchy on their triggers. And I felt a bit like Barry Manilow at the PLO Annual Dinner Dance – it was very strange. At the end of the song I took my bow and they didn't clap because it's not in their tradition to clap, but I think they liked it because they didn't kill me. So in honour of this performance they painted a snake on me with this red dye, and I asked what kind of snake it was, and they said it was a Pit Viper, a very rare snake and very powerful. It's a powerful symbol.

That night we went to sleep in hammocks strung between the trees and my girlfriend woke me up and she said, 'Sting, there's a snake.' I said, 'Go back to sleep, you're imagining it.' She said, 'No, I insist there *is* a snake.' So anyway I shone my torch and sure enough there it is, it's enormous, with its head reared up, and I said to her, 'What is it?' My girlfriend (she's an expert on snakes) said, 'It's a Pit Viper.' I said, 'What do they do?' She said, 'They jump ten feet and they kill you.' So I said, 'What do we do?' On either side of us are these warriors who were protecting us, and I said, 'Excuse me, Mr Warrior, there is a Pit Viper–' Ohh – they ran, these warriors, ran into the jungle and we were left standing, and I said, 'What do we do.' She said, 'Just stay still.'

Then the warriors came back with a big stick and they killed it.

Their explanation was that I was wearing the markings of this very snake and it's very rare that they come anywhere near humans. They said that the snake had come in tribute to me and it was going to give me power and everything. My friend, who is an anthropologist, said the real reason is that the snake wanted a warm body to get next to, it was cold – it kills you first then sleeps with you. So I owe my life to my girlfriend.

KEITH FLOYD I lived in a small market town in France and I became a kind of unofficial ambassador. For a start, they liked the fact that a Brit was actually living and working in their community as opposed to just coming along to rip off the grapes and the cherries and have a good time and pass by. But it did mean that if Liverpool beat the French at football they wouldn't speak to me for a week. If, as usual in the five years that I lived there, England lost every rugby match, they thought that was great and they made me walk around with the Union Jack at half mast in the bar. And when Lord Mountbatten was murdered it was the most extraordinary morning. It usually took me thirty seconds to walk up the road from my restaurant to the market square, and on that occasion it took me twenty minutes. All the older people came out of their houses and said, 'We are desolate, we are sorry that this happened to this man, you must feel very sad.'

DUDLEY MOORE Once I was in Majorca doing some publicity for a film and I was staying at the Plaza Hotel and I could not decide what to have – there was prime rib and veal cutlet and spinach and broccoli – I wanted everything, so I ordered for two people. I was on my own in this room, and the room service waiter came in with this gigantic table, so I went to the bathroom door which I had previously closed, and I knocked on it and said, 'Dinner is up, darling' – there was nobody in there, but I had a wonderful time all by myself.

A TASTE OF FOREIGN PARTS...

PETER USTINOV The most extraordinary dish that's ever been placed before me was in the poorest province of China, Gansu, where the average wage is something absolutely miserable, and where they're very courageous, very tough people, living in sand with nothing at all. The Governor of the State put a little dish in front of me which had something in it looking like India rubbers, enclosed in a kind of loose sauce, and he said, 'This, you've got to try.' Well, I didn't like the look of it frankly, but I put it in my mouth and it had the consistency of phlegm – which is not something you voluntarily put into your mouth. It not only looked like India rubber but it really tasted no more than an India rubber, and I couldn't understand *how* one could find it wonderful. I swallowed it with difficulty and then I asked him what it was and it turned out to be the pads on the bottom of a camel's feet. The sort of thing that your nanny would have said, 'Don't touch that! You never know where it's been!' And then in order to make conversation and to forget what I'd just eaten, I said, 'What do you do with the rest of the camel?' In this poorest province, he said, 'Nothing.' It was a tremendous delicacy – *only* the bottom of the feet.

JOHN CLEESE I think all food is good, except Mexican food. Have you ever eaten Mexican food? I think it should be made illegal. You get a great plate and it doesn't have anything on it except pools of different coloured things. You ask, 'What is this brown pile?' They say, 'That's re-fried beans, haven't you come across them?' Re-fried? Didn't they get them right the first time?

I LIKE TO BE IN AMERICA!

Oh, they're great in America. When I got married, it was all: 'Have a b-y-eautiful life, have a b-y-eautiful Christmas, have a b-y-eautiful New Year, have a b-y-eautiful home' – I mean, I didn't know these people. Everybody is a pure, beautiful person – and they think I'm a bit strange.

— Tracey Ullman

As a child I had one ambition that obsessed me more than any other – to visit America. It was a dream that started in the cinema, where I escaped from the grim austerity of the '30s and '40s and wallowed in the luxury of the American way. When I was evacuated to Somerset I was overjoyed to discover that a battalion of real live GIs were camped in the local meadows and I used to run errands for them and we got along fine. One GI, called Philip Demopoulos, even wanted to know if my parents would allow him to adopt me. One day I went down to the camp as usual and they'd gone. They left me a box, full of medals and buttons and things, and on the top they'd written: 'To Mike, from the boys. So long, kid, it was swell knowing you.'

When I was a little older, the man in the upstairs flat received a suit from an American cousin. It didn't fit him and he offered it to me. I did everything I could short of surgery to make that suit fit and it broke my heart not to be able to wear it. I even used to dream of America. I remember one particularly vivid one where I felt myself waking, and just grabbed at a pebble, something of America to hold on to, that I could bring from my dream and into my real life. I wanted to be there with my pals, Boston Blackie, the Bowery Boys, Abbott and Costello, and to wander the range with the sons of the pioneers.

I was 40 years old when I finally made it. In January 1973 I climbed aboard a Boeing 747 at Heathrow and within hours we were flying over America. When the pilot said that the lights of Boston were visible below I dropped everything and rushed to the other side of the aircraft to look. The feeling I got from seeing them was colossal. I remember thinking it didn't matter what happened to me afterwards, whether the plane crashed or we had to turn back, I'd seen America.

I stayed in New York, and taped the sounds of the traffic and the streets. I wasn't disappointed by any bit of it. I went to Hollywood and was the perfect tourist – gaping, taking pictures, buying mementoes and putting my feet in the footprints of the stars.

I even did a radio interview in San Francisco. The mother of a friend of mine who lived in America had sent in such a glowing report of me that I was invited on as a guest, but for once my timing was better than usual. The studio I was in was on the ground floor with windows on to the street – passers-by used to look in and wave. A week or so after I'd been there, there was a banging on the window. Everyone turned to see a man emptying his revolver at them. Thankfully the glass was soundproof and thick enough to protect them but the gunman ran around to the front door, and shot dead an executive of the company. A secretary was also killed before the man turned the gun on himself.

Back in London I got to know a man called Roy Fox. He was a band leader, in his late seventies. But he was, at one time, head of music at 20th Century Fox, and he had the most wonderful stories to tell. He told me about a blonde girl he'd met in the studio canteen. She was just a teenager, there with her mum to take a screen test. Roy even suggested a name for her, and they went out on a few dates. That blonde was Jean Harlow.

He told me that there was a small town between the studios and the beach, through which all the stars used to roar in the middle of the night, making a terrible row. Well, the mayor of this town had had enough of it, so he said, 'The next person who does that is going inside for a fortnight.' The next person was a popular star, Bebe Daniels, but imprisonment didn't turn out to be too much of a hardship for her. She had all her furniture moved into her cell, and Roy was instructed to take his orchestra outside the window and play to her. I liked that story. I wanted the stars to be barmy, crazy, and larger than life.

Many of the people I've talked to seem to find America beyond belief at times...

PAMELA STEPHENSON I love Hollywood. Every time I go to Hollywood I'm glad I live in Britain, but I still love it. It's a city of extremes, and when I'm there I do everything – I go mud wrestling and things like that. Last time I was there, I was staying in a hotel where they were having a conference on what to do when your shrink goes on holiday. I think they found me a bit unusual – mainly because of the way I look. I remember I went to a huge Hollywood party and they kept staring at me, because I was wearing black and bright orange and lime green. I swear there wasn't one other person there who wasn't wearing white and lilac. One day I got a Zen taxi driver. 'Well,' I said to him, 'how far is it to Laurel Canyon?' He said, 'Like, how deep is the Ocean...'

CLIVE JAMES We did a programme on the city of Dallas – you've got to realize they have a very high living standard there, which made me very nervous, especially in the hotel I was in. It was called the Mansion on Turtle Creek which some people say is the most expensive and certainly the most luxurious in the country. When I checked into my room, I'd never *seen* so many towels. I mean, one human being couldn't use all those towels – I thought they'd booked me in with a Symphony Orchestra.... And they had nouvelle cuisine breakfasts – sliced mangoes sprinkled with gold dust – it was just insane.

JACKIE COLLINS A Hollywood wife is a woman who gets up in the morning and if she has a broken nail, her day is ruined. She has a man who comes to the house and he stretches her body because that's very chic. She doesn't want to go to the gym with all the sweaty people, so she has him come to the house. Then her secretary will phone another Hollywood wife's secretary to make an appointment for lunch, and they'll go to a bistro and trash all their friends. Then they'll go for a little shop and buy a $6,000 or $7,000 dress. I had one acquaintance whom I bumped into the night before the Oscars, and she said, 'My God, Jackie, I just don't know what I'm going to wear, I've worn everything – I've got all these $3,000 and $4,000 dresses and I've worn them all.' So I looked at her, and I was kind of sending her up, and I said, 'Well, you know, you've always liked jewellery, why don't you just get new diamonds?' And she said, 'What a great idea!' Grace Robbins, who's married to Harold Robbins, has solid gold nails. They're *solid* gold. I said, 'My God, if you're ever robbed you'll be in trouble, they'll pull your nails off!' The jewellers act as the Hollywood grapevine – they know everything, because the Hollywood husband will go in and he'll order something wonderful for his wife, and something wonderful for the mistress – who's sometimes the wife's best friend. Then the Hollywood wife will go in and she'll order a lot of things and the jeweller says: 'Aha! There's going to be a divorce here in about two weeks.' And it's always true, because she goes in and stocks up like a squirrel before the divorce comes.

LULU Larry Hagman lives in Malibu and his home is all very Moorish, sort of Spanish style, with lots of wood and lots of stone, but everything is remote control. He has a roof which opens – it actually opens. I said, 'Fantastic, but what if it rains? You can't go out and leave the roof open.' And he said, 'Yes, you can.' They have a little thermometer that detects moisture in the air and the roof closes when it's going to rain. That tickled me pink!

BRITT EKLAND To live in LA you almost have to be successful now – at least have the visual things, the Rolls-Royce, the maids, the tennis court, those things. Of course, we don't know how much of all that they own because I was told that you can actually take your automobile and get a loan on it. You don't have to own that car, but you can still get a loan on it. I couldn't believe it. A lot of it, I think, is on very shaky ground.

DEBORAH KERR I think it's still fashionable to run Hollywood down. I was part of their fantastic publicity machine – they really made stars, they knew just how to do it. I mean, they made me a star. They did it by making sure that if you weren't acting in a movie, you were in the publicity department having pictures taken for the covers of magazines which don't exist any more.

ANTHONY HOPKINS I think the rule of the game when you live in Hollywood is to remember that it *is* a game. But it's not about money, it's about status and prestige and all that. And if you understand the rules you can have a pretty good life. I didn't get that involved. I went to a few awards ceremonies and a couple of parties and they were fine. I remember we went to one where they gave Bette Davis an award, and there was a great to-do and long speeches, and when they finally gave her the award, it fell to pieces in her hand! There is a shallowness, a glitziness about it, but if you accept it for what it is, it's all right. I think people take it too seriously. What I like about the Americans is that they don't apologize for anything, they say it straight. I was talking to a producer about the theatre once, and I said, 'I'm sorry to bother you   ' and he said, 'Why the hell are you sorry, do you want to know it or don't you?' I learned a lesson – don't apologize all the time. Admittedly they take rudeness to the point of lunacy but they do get on with it, they say it straight, as it is, and I think in this country we do tend to apologize too much for ourselves, and put ourselves down.

NEIL KINNOCK There are some things in America that I do admire. There aren't these terrific inhibitions that we have, related to accent, and where you're from and all the rest of it. The depressing things, of course, are the extremes of poverty that you see, because there's nothing resembling the safety net that we've got.

RUBY WAX My father always says that Miami is the only cemetery with a sea view. It's where all the old retirees go to die. They all sit around the pool waiting to die or eat, whichever comes first.

GLENDA JACKSON The very first time I went to Hollywood to work I was treated like royalty. I was there doing a film and it was awful – I walked on the set (and they had been working for two days before I got there) and it went totally quiet, and it was all 'Miss Jackson this' and 'Miss Jackson that' and I thought, 'I can't stand this,' because I can't work in this sort of atmosphere. So I swore loudly and frequently and after that it was all right. The odd four-letter word can get you out of some very sticky situations.

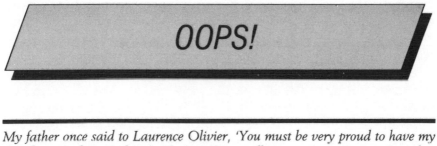

OOPS!

There's a horrible streak in all of us that loves to hear about other people's embarrassments, those excruciating moments that linger in the memory. I'm reluctantly reminded of a spring day in 1954, when I went to audition for BBC radio in Cardiff. There was a blind drawn over the studio window between me and my 'audience' in the control room so that they could concentrate on my voice without being distracted by my appearance.

At the given signal I began reading from one of my prepared pieces. After six words, the door opened and a man came in, grabbed me by the shoulders and spun me around – I'd been speaking with my back to the microphone. I imagine the report said 'Useful voice, poor sense of direction'.

Some of my guests' embarrassing moments have been not only horribly public, but captured for posterity on film or camera. . . .

VINCENT PRICE I'm awfully proud – there's a book out now of the fifty worst films ever made and one of them that I did is in it. It's called *Green Hell*, and it had Douglas Fairbanks Jr and a real bevy of stars in it, and I had a very small part – I was killed early on, thank God. This will give you a picture of the thing: we're in a little boat going down the Amazon, piranhas jumping all around us. And I turn to Doug Fairbanks Jr whose character's name is Brandy – that gives you a clue – and I say, 'Brandy, do you think it's possible for a man to be in love with two women at the same time? And in his heart to be faithful to each and yet want to be free of both of them?' The house came down. . . .

JOAN COLLINS The lowest point of my career has to be when I made *Empire of the Ants*. The title tells it all. I went off to the Florida swamps for six weeks just before Christmas and I played the role of a woman who gets lost in the jungle and is terrorized by giant, man-eating, seven-foot papier mâché ants. I was in the swamps up to my knees, having to fall all over the place and my legs were covered in cuts which became totally infected. It was really the lowest point of my life because to have a giant papier mâché ant fall on top of you and kill you with its noxious fumes is the most embarrassing and awful thing an actress can do. Shortly after that I decided I'd take off my clothes and do *The Stud* – it was preferable. I'd rather do porno than ants . . .

JULIE WALTERS I went on the Johnny Carson show in America twice in one week. He took a bit of a shine to me actually, did old Johnny. I'd gone over and they put me in very posh hotels, and I was met by a car that's bigger than my flat – really, I could have moved in there quite comfortably and my mother and Auntie Agnes as well, so I went on and on about that, and Johnny loved it. He loved it so much that he asked me to come back a couple of nights later, with Sammy Davis Junior, who was also a guest. He wanted me to go on about the Hollywood thing again, which was fine because my favourite subject was the Beverly Hills Hotel. It's like a pink cake, and I went on about the pool there, and the people all around it who were just covered in gold. I really did go on about it. 'All that gold's really ugly,' I said. 'Why don't they just wear their bank statements and a gold block on their heads?' I said. 'Those people, they dive into the swimming pool – it's a wonder they ever come up.' So anyway we had a bit of a laugh – in fact there were *gales* of laughter, so much so that I thought I'd put my dress on back to front or something. But anyway they were laughing and Johnny said, 'Sammy likes jewellery,' and I suddenly thought, 'Oh yes, he does!' So Sammy showed me his hand, and he had some quite tasteful rings on, and I said, 'No, Sammy, I'm not talking about that kind of thing . . .' And then he showed me the other hand, and down came enough gold to revive the British economy! I've never been on the Johnny Carson show since.

PAMELA STEPHENSON I came pretty unstuck a while ago. I was doing an award ceremony and I was presenting an award with a man called Chuck Norris who's a sort of white Bruce Lee. Now it's well known that these events can be really boring because you get this terrible dialogue that's written for you. Like, 'Well, Pamela, I wonder who's going to win tonight,' and, 'Yes, Chuck, I can't wait to hear the outcome.' Anyway, I decided that we'd do this routine where I was going to come on in a karate suit and throw him, Kung Fu style, and he was then going to say, 'No woman treats me like that,' and pull my karate suit off to reveal my evening dress. However, we rehearsed it about three times and it started getting terribly stale so I decided that the best thing to do was to remove the dress just before I went on. It was a terrible, terrible mistake, because when it came to it, and he actually pulled off my karate suit, he got such a shock that he just left me there, centre stage, while he beetled off. So there I was, standing there with the karate suit wrapped around my legs, having to bunny hop and crawl off stage, very slowly, with millions of people watching. Oh God, it was so embarrassing!

BERYL REID I was at the National Theatre and finding your way in and out was the most daunting thing about it, because you could get lost anywhere, though I must say I made a lot of friends asking the way. On my first day there I got to the dressing-room all right because somebody took me there, and then I started looking for the rehearsal room. Well, I had no idea really – I just knew I had to look for these lights. In the end I *saw* some lights, and I walked through a door, and on to what I took to be our rehearsal stage. I looked across and saw a lot of people in gold, acting their knickers down, but then when I looked around, I thought, 'Oh my God, there's the audience!' Of course, what had happened was that I'd wandered on to the proper stage at the National, with a play in full flood, and me with my shopping basket and very old black trousers and sweater and a rehearsal face, if you know what I mean. Albert Finney was acting on the other side of the stage and I thought, now the thing is not to hurry off – hurry? I wanted to run! But I thought, no, *I'll stroll* off. Poor old Albert Finney never even knew I'd been on, and it was the only performance I didn't get paid for.

WENDY CRAIG Once I had to appear at a Methodist Youth rally at the Albert Hall – a very grand occasion, you see. So I bought myself a very elegant black dress, made of pure silk, and very sheer. When the time came I had to make a grand entrance with all the lights blazing and I was bowing and waving and being frightfully queenly, you know, as only I can be. I thought I'd done very well, and then I was sent photographs of the event afterwards, and the lights had shone right through my dress and you could see my bra, my girdle, my suspenders...

DAVID FROST The trickiest interview I ever did was with the world's greatest talking bird, from Toronto in Canada. This bird's trainer was a very pushy chap called Colin, and he kept saying, 'Go on, David, ask him any question, go on.' And I said, 'I will, if only you'll shut up.' So eventually he did keep quiet and I did a five minute interview with this bird – without getting a single peep out of him, not a sound, not a dicky bird. So I said, 'This is the world's greatest mime artist among talking birds, the Marcel Marceau of talking birds.' It was a total plonker.

MARGARET THATCHER At the House of Commons you can always have a *double entendre* and you really have to be very careful. My first junior ministerial job was with Harold Macmillan and I was a Parliamentary Secretary to the Minister of Pensions. I worked very hard and I learnt all my statistics, and then I went round to all the pensioners' organizations. Now, I'd done all the figures but people just didn't think that one of them was right, so I sent someone to the Civil Service to check. And my mind was on the job, as it would be, and along came a piece of paper out of the dispatch box. I picked it up, looked at it, and announced: 'I have the latest red hot figure...'

GHASTLY GAFFES AND SOCIAL BLUNDERS....

DENIS NORDEN Of course gaffes are worse in real life than on film because you can't retake. A lot of mine happen in bathrooms and places like that. I'm sure it must be a fairly common male experience where you go to a strange house and you use their loo, and find that when you wash your hands, the tap runs faster than the one you've got at home, and it just goes SPLASH all over the front of your trousers. Obviously you can't possibly go downstairs like that so you stand there for ages, and you keep hearing these little footsteps outside, and voices saying: 'Are you all right, in there?'

BILLY CONNOLLY I once heard a story about a guy who was staying in someone's house and in the middle of the night, he needed a pee, but he didn't know where the loo was. So he grabbed a vase from the mantelpiece and did it in there. Then he left the house, and everything was fine and he forgot all about it, until some months later, the host came up to him and said, 'I don't ever want to speak to you again – you peed in the remains of my uncle Harry.'

VICTORIA WOOD My husband and I once arranged to meet up in the car park on the motorway service station and luckily enough, I spotted his van in the corner when I got there, and I saw through the windscreen that he was sitting in the car reading the paper. So I went up and sat on the bonnet – which I probably dented – and I peered through the glass and said, 'Do you fancy a good time, big boy?' And it wasn't him.

Julie Walters and I once went to see a pantomime and we were sitting in the audience and a great buzz went around, with everyone looking at us. So we went very red but we got out our pens and we were all ready, poised to sign a few autographs, but it wasn't us they were looking at, at all. It was Mike Read, the DJ, who was sitting four seats back.

ROBBIE COLTRANE The last time I was in New York I went to this bar on the lower West Side and it really is one of these 'three previous convictions before you're allowed' in type bars, and the guy who serves there is very calculating and very camp and I was wearing my tartan suit at the time – low profile, very low profile – and I was just waiting. I said, 'Give us a drink,' and he went, 'You are not having a drink.' And I was a bit embarrassed and I said, 'Why not?' And he said, 'You know perfectly well why not.' And I spent the whole of the evening thinking, 'What did I do last time I was here?' It was three years previously. Only history will tell. It hasn't come back to me yet – but I believe no windows were left intact.

SEAN CONNERY I'm terrified of needles. In fact, the first cartilage operation I had was because I knelt on a needle. It was sticking out of the carpet with the eye of the needle pointing up with the thread in it, and it went in my knee and took ages to get out. When I was younger, they had the diphtheria epidemic in Scotland and everybody had to go and have these inoculations which were in three stages and apparently they got worse and worse – you know what's it like when you're a kid. And I was standing behind this girl called Cathy Logan – she was so big, her arm was like my leg – and they put the needle right in the biceps – and that's the last thing I remember. I've been the same with needles ever since.

SU POLLARD I've had some lean times – and the leanest of all was quite humiliating. I was in a café, I was about nineteen and hadn't been working for a while because I'd had flu. I'd left home by this time and never had any money – and if I did get some I'd blow it on a pair of trousers or something. Anyway, this particular time, I got a sausage sandwich in a café. That's all I could afford, but there was a bloke behind me who had two chops and a salad. When he got up to go, I noticed that he'd left a chop, so thought, 'Marvellous!' grabbed it and ate it. But a few minutes later he came back in. My dear, I thought I would die! Of course he was looking everywhere for this chop, under the chair, under the plate. And I was thinking, 'God, it's in my stomach!' It was mortifying – but it makes me laugh.

THE YOLK'S ON THEM...

JULIE ANDREWS It's fun shocking people. There was a lovely time when I was with Carol Burnett – she's a good friend who brings out the best and the worst in me, I think. We were doing a gala for President Johnson in Washington and we were up in our rooms, waiting for Mike Nichols to arrive. Finally he called and said, 'I'm coming right away – order me some coffee, I'll be right there.' So we decided to go to the elevator to greet him, and while we were waiting for the elevator, we had this great idea. 'Let's do something funny,' we said. 'Let's be kissing as he gets out of the elevator.' So I flung Carol down in a deep embrace, and the elevator went 'ping', the doors opened – but it was filled with secret service men. Carol just dropped to her knees and disappeared behind the couch! Eventually the elevator went 'ping' again, and we thought, well this has *got* to be him, so we flung ourselves into this idiot embrace and the doors open, and it's – Lady Bird Johnson! She got out and went down the corridor and then she stopped – you could see she was thinking, 'I know those people...' So she came back and she said to Carol, 'Excuse me, aren't you Carol Burnett?' And Carol said, 'Yes – and this is my friend Mary Poppins!' Eventually, to our mortification, the elevator finally went 'ping', and it *was* Mike Nichols, but he just got out of the elevator, saw us locked in this passionate clinch, and said, 'Oh hi, girls' and walked on down the corridor!

DENNIS TAYLOR All the snooker players play little tricks on each other – in fact I owe Steve Davis one. We used to go to a private house in Eastbourne and play exhibitions – this is going back a good few years now. Well, we'd been there that many times that on one occasion, Graham Miles and myself decided to dress up as two lady snooker champions. We put on the full regalia, the wig, the make-up, and I stuffed two large apples down my jumper to complete the effect – which wasn't easy, I can tell you, I'll never forget that first shot – and we were introduced as two Lancashire lady snooker champions. Anyway we took a photograph and I forgot all about it until I was watching *A Question of Sport* one day and up it flashed on the television screen. Steve Davis had got hold of a copy and sent it into them.

NORMAN TEBBIT I never rode my motorbike very fast – it wouldn't go very fast. But I was the victim of a plot – you know how politicians are often victims of plots – it happened to me from a very young age. I was persuaded that I could ride my motorcycle upstairs. What I didn't know was that my friends – I use this expression very loosely – had loosened the clips on the stair carpet. So as I was about half-way up I was conscious of having to use more and more throttle to hold off the inevitable and awful moment when motorcycle and I and stair carpet all finished up at the bottom of the stairs.

NICHOLAS LYNDHURST We work pretty hard on *Only Fools and Horses* – we're up very early and we're working till late at night and then when we do get a day off, it's usually a Sunday when everything's shut. But there was one occasion when we were filming down in Dorset and we had Sunday off and we all shot over to Poole, where everything was shut except for this joke shop where they sold these incredibly·realistic pools of plastic sick. So of course I bought one, and then later on, I arranged to meet David Jason down in the hotel bar. I left the sick outside his bedroom door, because his room was directly opposite mine, and I was squinting through the keyhole waiting for him to come out and say, 'Oh gosh, there's some sick, how dreadful,' and thinking how wonderful and wacky that would be. The only trouble was that David was already downstairs in the hotel bar . . .

CLAIRE RAYNER I was a theatre staff nurse for a while, you know, standing there handing bits and bobs to the surgeon. And we had a marvellous surgeon, a wonderful man whose speciality was rectal surgery. His name was Gabriel, so inevitably he was known as the arse angel! During one of his operations, the consultant anaesthetist was getting a little bored, because the patient was happily asleep, and so he kept filling up a syringe and squirting it at my legs. Anyway, at the end of a very long operation, Gabriel stripped off his gloves, stepped back, and there, around my feet, was this vast puddle. And he just looked at me and said: 'Really, nurse, you could have asked.'

WE ARE A PARENT

Every night I whisper to my son, 'Entrepreneur, entrepreneur ...' I hope he'll take care of me in my old age.

— Ruby Wax

I'm in my fifties now, and I've come to the conclusion that this is the right time to become a parent. When you're younger, you're busy trying to make your way and keep your head above water. When you're older, all you want to do is be with them.

I've been a father to six children. My eldest two, Greg and Richard, were from my first marriage. When Greg was seven and Richard five, they all went to live in Australia. Edward and Jane are from my second marriage. They're twins, and like all of the children, not very interested in what I do — which doesn't mean they don't care for me.

My youngest two, Patrick and Daniel, are still children, and I have a grandson only four years younger than Daniel. I seem to worry more about the children now that I'm older, but then I suppose that there was more to worry about with Patrick. He was born with cerebral palsy and for the first eight months, we simply didn't know if he would live. When we passed that crisis, we worried about how he would get on, and wondered if he would ever even sleep through a whole night. The first seven years were exhausting, but I think because of that, I've been obsessed with Patrick. I loved him instantly. He is unable to use his left hand very well, and in the early days, when he was tiny, his fist was clenched tightly shut. One day as I sat with him I found that my left fist was clenched as well. Apart from his slight physical problems he is a bright and handsome little boy with an innate skill with words – must get it from his mother.

And Daniel is like something from a Mabel Lucy Atwell book, chubby, huge eyed, boisterous.

Being the child of a well-known parent is something I wouldn't wish on anybody. I think it gives them an extra hurdle. Sometimes people expect more of them, just because of their name, others are deliberately rude, just for the sake of it. Like saying, 'I think your father's a load of rubbish,' a quite permissible point of view but not something children wish to hear.

Daniel came up to me recently and in a disgruntled voice said, 'Someone told me I was famous, today – I'm not, you are.' If I were David Jason I think they'd be immensely proud, because he's the voice of Toad and Danger Mouse. I think they've got their priorities right.

These are a few views on parenthood I've gleaned during the series . . .

ANNE DIAMOND Motherhood is lovely but it's very tiring. Everybody told me your life changes completely and I thought, 'Yes, yes . . .' but of course it has happened. Suddenly you've got to embrace a whole new world – you've got nannies and their problems, and their relatives, and their boyfriends ringing up at night. Suddenly your life has expanded tremendously, but it's good fun.

PAMELA STEPHENSON They tell you that having a baby is supposed to be a spiritual experience – you're supposed to gaze into its eyes when you're feeding it and all that – well, I just can't believe that a thing that small makes a noise like that. I had huge knockers when I was breast feeding – they just grew so much, I thought, 'Watch out, Dolly Parton.' I've become the most overprotective mum – I'm so scared about germs that before I breast-feed her I boil my nipples.

MAUREEN LIPMAN They're nicely eccentric, the kids. Adam has just come out of what we call his Burgess and Maclean phase, where he's been looking over his shoulder the whole time. We were very worried about it – we thought he had some neurological problem. Finally it emerged that he'd heard that God was everywhere. He didn't want to miss him, you see.

I do have an au pair to help me along, and I have an understanding husband. My latest au pair is from Australia – I've been through this language business so many times that I thought, 'This time, I'll get someone who speaks English.' So I put an advert in an Australian paper and I was inundated with replies. I went through them all and they all seemed wonderful. But I chose the lady whom I've got now because she'd been working in a nursery for two and a half years, so I thought she must be OK. So we went through the formalities and she came over and after a day or two, I said to her, 'Sandy, how long were you working in the nursery?' and she said, 'Oh, two and a half years.' And I said, 'How many children did you have in your charge?' 'Pardon?' she said. So I said, 'How many children were you looking after?' And she said, 'No, not children – plants!'

ALAN BATES I've got identical twins, except that they're not identical, if you know what I mean. When I took them out to their first restaurant, I said to them, 'What will you have?' One said, 'I think I'll have the snails and then I'll have quails, please.' The other one said, 'Steak and chips, please.' Quite a difference, isn't there!

MARGARET THATCHER I didn't know I was having twins until the day they were born – they arrived six or seven weeks early, as sometimes happens with twins, and it wasn't terribly easy, and the doctor suddenly said to me: 'I think there are two there . . .' And I remember saying, 'Well, I hope you can get both of them.' They both have very strong personalities and I turn to them for advice and, of course, they'll turn to me, as well. Carol is on television sometimes, and sometimes she's on radio, and often she takes over at very difficult times – Christmas Day and Boxing Day. I remember she was doing a phone-in show from about 10 in the evening until two in the morning – and there comes a time when you don't really get people phoning at that time. So as she left, I said to her, 'If you're short of telephone calls, dear, just phone me.' And just after midnight, she called and said, 'Mum, I've run out.' I said, 'Don't worry, I'll keep you going for twenty minutes . . .'

JAN FRANCIS When my little daughter was two I showed her the list of runners in the Grand National, and a chubby finger went out and picked one. So we put on three pounds and it came up – she won forty-something pounds. We tried her again this year – it didn't work.

KIRK DOUGLAS I have four sons and they're all in the business. Michael, of course, is doing well – maybe when things slacken off he might think of political ambitions, but I doubt that for the moment. As a matter of fact, Michael really annoys me a little bit. When I think of all the struggling I've gone through – and I guess we've all gone through it – Michael suddenly came along and had four or five hits in a row. But I will say this – I once wrote him a note and said, 'Michael, I'm more proud of how you handle your success than I am of your success,' because he's a good guy.

DENNIS TAYLOR The most important thing to me is my wife and family. Whether you win your snooker match or you lose, it's nice to be able to go back home again. If you win, it's all celebrations, if you lose, it's nothing to bother about because the children aren't interested anyway – they're talking about what they did at school that day.

TELLY SAVALAS I shaved my head for a motion picture called *The Greatest Story Ever Told* – the life of Jesus. And the director says, 'Telly, I'd like you to shave your head, how do you feel about that?' 'Well, if the money's right, I don't care,' I said, 'but I've got little kids at home, and I think it would be traumatic for them if I just showed up looking so different.' So the director said 'OK, we'll put off filming for a day and they can come in tomorrow and watch it being done.' Honestly, my kids never even noticed. Now if I let my hair grow I'll scare them to death!

PAUL McCARTNEY My children tell me they like my music but I think it's just to stay up late. The way we play it in our family is that I'm not famous – I'm just Dad. I don't look at all famous in our house. We keep it like that on purpose because I'm pretty well-known and it could go to their heads. When they were very little, one of the kids came up and said, 'You're Paul McCartney.' But it's Dad normally, and Paul McCartney is that fellow we see on telly.

YOKO ONO I think Sean should have the freedom of growing in the way he wants to grow, but I'm also very caring about him – making sure that he's healthy and knows what's what. But that's something that's very interesting about Sean's generation. They're very careful, caring and health-oriented. I don't think we really have to worry much about the future generation.

DAVID STEEL I think it's very important to take holidays as a family, particularly in politics. When the children were younger, we used to have a Land Rover dormobile, with a roof that went up at the top and bunks that came out at the side. And when we had the first two children, they used to be put to sleep there, having just had their dinner of baked beans or whatever, and then Judy would cook the most marvellous meal for the two of us. I remember one occasion very vividly – it was in Austria, underneath the mountains and we had a bottle of wine on the table, a wonderful fillet steak in front of us, and I was just putting my knife into it when I felt a drip on the top of my head – my daughter had peed in the bed up above.

TWIGGY My daughter Carly thinks all mums and dads sing and dance and get on a stage. She's very long and thin – she's got better legs than me. All my life I've moaned about my legs because they were so skinny so I think whoever's up there watching us gave her the legs I always wanted. They're great.

RINGO STARR I keep everything – I'm a hoarder – and I saved all my clothes through the years because I thought the kids would like them. But the only time they ask for any is if there's a fancy dress party.

GERMAINE GREER I have a special relationship with my godchildren and they do ask me for advice. But generally, the correct thing to do when you're asked for advice is not to give it, but to find out a little bit more about the problem and then usually the young person comes up with a sensible solution. The most important thing I can do as a godmother is just to listen. If you're a mother, you get too emotionally involved and too frightened for what might happen to the children. But godmothers are further removed, and I love being a godmother – it's really a gas.

OUT OF THE MOUTHS OF BABES...

CLAIRE RAYNER When my son was about three, I was having this wonderful Saturday morning treat that mothers sometimes have – a bath – and he was toddling in and out. After a while, he leaned over the side of the bath to have a little chat, and he leaned forward and with one finger very delicately touched each boob, and said, 'I do like those – did you knit them?'

BOB GELDOF It's unfortunate because my daughter Fifi looks like me, and behaves like Paula, and it's completely the wrong way round. She is like any three-year-old – she is very wilful and it is absolutely outrageous to find yourself arguing with a three-year-old. And then you have to throw away all your sophistication and you say, 'Because I'm older, that's why.' She has these notions of what older people do; she said, 'Hey Dad, you know what grown-ups do at their parties?' And I said, 'No.' And she said, 'They stay up very late and dance a lot and they eat jelly.' And that is exactly what a lot of the parties I go to are like.

GEORGE HARRISON My nine-year-old son has become aware of my past in the last few years, although I didn't really tell him anything about the Beatles because it was so long ago. Anyway I didn't want to burden him with all that. Nevertheless I think most kids when they get to about four or five see *Yellow Submarine*, and then he sort of twigged. But he wasn't impressed. He came to a show I did for the Prince's Trust last July and afterwards, I said to him 'What did you think?' and he said, 'Oh yeah, you were OK, Dad – why didn't you do "Rock 'n' Roll Music" and "Sweet Little Sixteen" and "Johnny B. Good"?' So I said, 'Actually, that's Chuck Berry.'

GARY WILMOT Katy, my eldest child, is three and she says such wonderful things – she's just finding her own personality and she's got a great sense of humour. I did a pantomine at Christmas and she came to see it a few times, and my wife was on the phone a few days ago to her mother in Southend, and her mum said, 'I've got some bad news, did you hear about Aunt Eve, she's fallen over and broken her leg', and my wife says, 'Oh no – she didn't', and Katy's voice came: 'Oh yes, she did!'

JUDGING BY APPEARANCES

I'll tell you what bothers me about age – it's people asking me if the thought of ageing bothers me.

— Julie Christie

There's no doubt that the body tends to head in a southerly direction as time goes on. I've read that some faces drop as much as six inches in ten years, which could be rather worrying if it went on for the next thirty years. I know that Yoko Ono, for one, believes that one's appearance is all in the mind anyway. We were discussing her stature. I asked her how tall she was. And she said, 'Very tall . . .' She was sitting there at five foot nothing or whatever, but in her mind she was eye to eye with Jerry Hall.

When I first became a TV announcer I was twenty-four but I looked about sixteen. When someone suggested my name as a compère for *Come Dancing*, the reply was, 'I don't think his mother would let him out so late.'

I know a lot of people my present age and even younger have had a few nips here and a few tucks there. I haven't considered it and I'm not sure that I ever would, but it's interesting how people don't think twice about having their teeth fixed but can get very righteous about having their flesh tampered with. Perhaps with my baggy eyes I have more reason than most to think about surgery. It's partly to do with having a slightly wonky kidney, but everyone assumes that bags under the eyes are caused by doing something disgusting. I've had them all my life, long before I started getting disgusting. No-one else in the family has them, just me, the one who's on television. That, you might say, is the way the cookie crumbles.

When I was younger I used to be ferociously fit. I ran, I swam a lot, played a poor game of tennis, and did a lot of rowing. The only problem with muscle is that when you stop the exercise that put it there in the first place, it doesn't just fade into your body, it heads down the outside – not a pretty sight. Grey hair doesn't bother me, as long as it keeps growing. No, I don't – and I wouldn't – wear a hair piece in spite of some scurrilous rumours to that effect.

One of the great advantages of getting older is that you don't have to try so hard. You can sit back and watch other people trying, instead. Nevertheless, I remember 32 as a very good age – for reasons which are none of your business. At 41 I'd begun to look mature but I was still very fit and I remember thinking I wouldn't mind freezing time for a while. One day you just look different in the mirror – something that you'd always recognized in yourself has gone. It's a bit disturbing when it happens but you live with it. It comes to us all if we're lucky.

Coming to terms with one's age and appearance is a universal problem, although you wouldn't think so to look at some of my guests . . .

JOAN COLLINS You cannot do anything about the fact that every May 23rd, I'm going to have a birthday – nothing's going to change that. So rather than try to hide it, I make a celebration out of it every year, and I enjoy it. Life isn't a rehearsal, this is it, and it's got to be as good as it can be. So I work very hard and I play very hard and I do try to do a lot of things.

I did that *Playboy* centrefold for a particular reason – I have so many women over forty coming up to me and thanking me, saying that I changed their lives after that. I think I showed that there is life after forty – I think that most actresses are over forty now in any case. Whereas when I first came into the business, I was only 16 or 17, and I was told I'd better make all the money I could because by the time I was 24 or 25 I'd be washed up. They really did think that.

I'm quite careful with what I eat – I don't eat a lot of meat and I don't eat a lot of fried things, or buns and cakes and crisps. I try to eat vegetables and salads . . . and I drink quite a lot of champagne.

BRITT EKLAND My age? Well, I'm getting a little too old to be playing Swedish au pair girls and a little too young for *Dynasty*.

DUSTIN HOFFMAN For the last twelve years, I've woken up with my wife and asked her, 'Am I too old to play Hamlet?' A week ago she finally said yes – I think that's a tough one.

TWIGGY I don't worry about getting older at the moment – maybe if we meet in twenty years' time I'll be crying on your shoulder – but at the moment it doesn't worry me. I like being the age I am because I'm much more confident and I can deal with things. I like being a mum and being the age I am because I can help my daughter, Carly.

CLIFF RICHARD Am I beginning to fray at the edges? I think most of me is, actually, I'm just a very good actor. I've faked it for a lot of years, and if you don't come too close, it's okay.

OMAR SHARIF I think I'm enjoying my age. First of all I'm starting a whole new career, so I'm looking forward to all the character parts I'll be playing. I was never young really, not inside of me. I always hated young juvenile lead parts. I hated to be the young lover in films. I always wanted to be older. I was never totally comfortable when I was a young man, but I'm totally comfortable now – finally.

MARGARET THATCHER I am never ill. I'll tell you the secret – I usually take Vitamin C every morning. I don't have breakfast, I take Vitamin C in some very nice sparkling water.

MICHAEL HORDERN One of the great things about our profession is that you can go on working when you're in your dotage – well, maybe not dotage, you've got to use a little up there. But if I were in any other profession, I'd have been retired fifteen years ago, but with acting, not only can I go on working, I'm jolly useful. Instead of finding a splendid actor of 40 and putting lines all over his face, they get the real thing without any trouble.

I was once doing a television programme with Finlay Currie who must have been in his eighties or nineties, then. This play called for a young teenage girl to play a very small part, but because her part was so small, she wasn't called to any rehearsals until right at the end of the rehearsal period, by which time the rest of the company had been together for three weeks, and all knew each other very well. On the afternoon the girl was called, we'd all just come back from lunch, and the door opened, and in came this absolutely smashing girl, and Finlay took one look at her and said, 'Oh to be 70 again . . .'

GLENDA JACKSON When I get old I'm going to work towards the 'eccentric old bat' end of the range. I intend to use to my advantage the hypocrisy that surrounds old age and I intend to insist that people give me a seat on the bus, and to stop the traffic, even though the lights are green and all that. I'm going to linger on pelican crossings for hours . . .

DENIS NORDEN I think my ambition is to become a dirty old man – but I need about five more years' training.

PETER USTINOV I've always made it one of my aims, even when I was quite small, to reach the year 2000. As it's getting awfully close, I'm now planning to reach 2005.

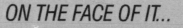

ON THE FACE OF IT...

JILL GASCOINE I never wash my face with soap and water. And I have never, ever, in my life, gone to bed with my make-up on, even at the most passionate times. I always get up afterwards and take the make-up off. I have to think myself into looking good, and I do work quite hard at it. For instance, I look dreadful in the mornings. You know that feeling when you get up in the morning and your face is still hanging on the end of the bed – oh, someone's clapping, they know exactly what I mean!

ANNEKA RICE When I was about eighteen, a producer needed a presenter to do a pilot for a children's programme called *On The Farm* or something. So he whisked me off to Wales for the weekend – no, not one of those weekends – we did a pilot, and I thought it went OK, but a week later, he called me into his office and said, 'I hate to be brutish about this but you haven't got a career in television, you've got a funny face.' He thought I had a real crisis with my teeth and he said, 'Go and get your teeth fixed.' He actually wrote to the head of the department saying, 'I have to put this formally because I know Anneka's very keen to do something in front of the camera, but if I was you, I'd stop it here and now – there's no hope.'

CHARLOTTE RAMPLING When I was eighteen I had an agent who said, 'But my dear, your eyes are completely uncommercial, they're completely unmodern. The eyes of nowadays are very wide-awake, very open – fresh-faced and clear like Jean Shrimpton and Twiggy. You're eyes are too hooded and threatening. Perhaps you could do with a bit of lifting...' Well, I know a lot of women think about lifting at some stage in their lives, but I was eighteen years old. Absurd!

MAUREEN LIPMAN When I first left drama school I was taken out by an American agent and he said, 'I saw your performance last night, take off your coat and show me your figure.' So I took it off, and showed him it, and he said, 'OK, put it back.' And then he said, 'Now, I think you have a big career in front of you, but I want you to take this piece of paper, and I want you to walk round to this office in Harley Street, and talk to the doctor about having a nose job.' And before I knew it, I was out of that office, and walking down the street, and actually in the offices of this Harley Street plastic surgeon. But then about three days before I was due to go in and have it done, it suddenly occurred to me that I could change my agent with less pain than I could change my nose – so I stuck with it.

CHARLTON HESTON I suppose one of my most valuable physical attributes, and one which has actually got me parts, came about by accident. My nose was broken from a failed career in school football. I wasn't a good player – that's why I got my nose broken, I suppose, but it actually turned out better than it was before. It was just a long nose before, but it's not a bad nose, now.

KENNETH WILLIAMS My nostrils are only like this because I played football in the Army. I didn't want to play, I hate exercise, I loathe it, and I've avoided it ever since, but on this occasion, a boot met my nose and it was chucked right out of joint. Some time afterwards, a surgeon said to me, 'You know, if it had been pressed back when the bone was manageable, you'd have got it back into the proper shape.' But it wasn't and consequently I've got this nose.

LAUREN BACALL I never was a great beauty and I never was a great sex symbol, I never had a great figure ... The famous smouldering look that I had actually came out of nerves. I was so nervous when I was in *To Have And Have Not* that I shook – I still shake, but not quite as badly – and then my head shook and in order to hold it still I had to put my head down, and rest my chin on my chest, and then I'd look up, and out of all that, came 'The Look'. It's really quite an unromantic story ...

DENIS HEALEY I think good looks are a slight disadvantage – for example, if you've got beautiful golden hair, and obviously wear a hair net in bed like Michael Heseltine ... On the whole, I think people like the craggy type with eyebrows – like me. When I was younger, they were fairly regular and they went right across and joined here in the middle. Now they turn up at the edge like horns and however hard I try to keep them down, within a few minutes, they're pointing up again.

HAIR PIECES....

ALAN COREN I gave my hair as a hostage to fortune. If you go hard of hair rather than totally bald at a fairly early age you come to terms with the fact that it is part of an ageing process and once that's happened – it happened to me about twenty-eight – you don't actually look as though you're getting very much older. Whereas if you're going to have to go white next, that's going to be a hell of a shock. The actual process of getting older doesn't bother me in the slightest.

FIONA FULLERTON It was my idea to be a brunette in *The Charmer*, because I wanted the character to look quite hard, and so I dyed my hair. It was extraordinary the difference it made – I just felt that people were talking to me in a very different way. I remember I was sitting on a committee during last summer when we were filming, at the first meeting I was a brunette, and everything went perfectly. I made several salient points and everybody accepted what

I was saying and said, 'Yes indeed, thank you, Miss Fullerton.' About three months later, we had another meeting and I'd finished filming by that time and gone back to being blonde, and it was if I wasn't there. Nobody listened to a word I had to say.

HARRISON FORD The film studio attempted to make me into 'something' – I don't know what they had in mind but they asked me to have my hair styled like Elvis Presley. They sent me down to the barber with an actual photograph of Elvis and someone to make sure that I went through with it. It didn't work out very well . . .

JOHN CLEESE I think I'm just awkward – I move strangely. You described me as moving like a cross between a giraffe and a hovercraft, but the first time I ever saw myself on television, in 1964, I couldn't believe it. It's like when you first hear your voice on a tape recorder and you think, 'That's not me!' The bottom half of me moved around on this cushion of air! When I moved like that as Basil Fawlty, people said, 'Gosh, doesn't he move funnily?' but that's just the way I walk. I regard my height as normal, you see, that's the trouble. My mother is only five foot one inch, incidentally, and when I was about 13 years of age – I was six foot tall at that point – people used to nudge each other as we went by.

I have no teeth at all now. Three fell out in a restaurant. I was talking to my dentist a little while ago, and I said, 'I do have one tooth left that's my own,' and he had a glance, and he said, 'No, that went two years ago.' So apart from my three hair transplants that I've had, I'm going to have some tooth implants because I'm told I'm a sex-symbol now and if I have the teeth implanted, I should be able to chew on both sides of my mouth, which I gather is essential for a sex symbol.

I've had three hair transplants and the transplanted hair is falling out. But toupees are just terrible, aren't they? We did a sketch once on *Monty Python* which I adored, about a man going into the toupee department, and when he arrived, three assistants came over to him with dead squirrels on their heads. And they all went on about how wonderful toupees were, and how you absolutely can't spot them at all. And one of them said, 'You may not believe this, but one of us is actually *wearing* a toupee . . .' and the man said, 'I thought all three of you were,' and they all rushed off to the mirror and started checking.

I think I'd draw the line at plastic surgery, but I'd certainly get knee transplants if there was any chance of that. But no, I think I've gone about as far as I can go.

WITH A LITTLE HELP FROM MY FRIENDS...

GERMAINE GREER I'm going to have a knee lift – it's all very well, but my knees are four inches lower than they were in the '50s.

DAME EDNA EVERAGE I believe in cosmetic surgery and I recommend it to a lot of people. In fact my bridesmaid had herself landscaped.

LIZA MINNELLI I don't really think about my appearance much. I don't think it's the way you look so much as what's going on inside you. I'm quite pleased with the way I look – I haven't had plastic surgery. You know, you can do anything now, it's quite miraculous. I saw Phyllis Diller, who's an American comedienne, and I swear to God I thought it was Cheryl Ladd – mind you when she smiles she has to cross her legs.

JOAN RIVERS Plastic surgery? What haven't I had done! I had my nose thinned and my eyes done which, no offence Michael, you could use a touch of. With a woman, everything just starts to go. Last night my brassiere was on the floor and my boobs were still in it.

WEIGHTY MATTERS....

PATRICK MOORE Somebody once told me that I give every impression of having been somewhat hastily constructed. I'm not prepared to deny this – I must be a tailor's nightmare. My trouble is that I weigh three stone more than I ought to, not because I eat too much – I don't – but because my thyroid doesn't work. It really doesn't matter that much.

DOLLY PARTON About four years ago I gained a lot of weight. I had a lot of female problems, and I had to have surgery and I knew then that I was never going to be able to have children. That was a really hard thing for me because I'd tried for them ever since I've been married, and I've been with my husband for twenty-three years. I made a statement to the Press about how I understood how people become suicidal and could resort to drugs and alcohol to ease the pain, and out of that came stories that I'd actually tried to kill myself. It wasn't as close as that but my spirit was a bit broken. Now I've got things in order in my life. I've lost about 50 pounds in weight, but I didn't go on a crash diet – it actually took me about three-and-a-half years to get the weight down. But I've been lucky in that I'm still in proportion – I'm just a miniature version of what I was. My waist has always been small – even when I was heavier that always saved me, and at the moment, it's about 19 inches, I guess. But I'm a little person, you see. I'm only five feet one – five feet two if I'm standing really tall – and for my height I'm a good weight now, about 107 pounds. I feel like I've been let out of prison now that I've finally got my weight down and been able to maintain it. Because I hate to diet, I hate diet food, I hate diet drinks. I love to eat what I like, when I like.

ROY KINNEAR You've got to be slightly careful about the roles you choose, in the theatre especially, because you've got to do it every night – if you're bad on the first night you know you're going to be bad again the next night, and eventually you're just bad all the time and everyone knows you're going to be bad because they've read the notices as well. You go out in the evenings and say, 'Bye bye, darling, I'm just going to be bad.' And you get home at night – 'Hello darling, were you bad again?' - 'Yes, thanks.'

I never actually take a part because the character's fat. The director says, 'How do you see this character?' and I say, 'Well, I see him as short, fat, bald.' And he says, 'Oh, that's a good idea. I never thought of him like that.'

VICTORIA WOOD I went on a hard-boiled egg and bacon diet once. There was some theory that hard-boiled eggs eat the food inside you – but it didn't work

HARRY SECOMBE Originally I lost five stones and I looked a bit haggard so I put about a stone-and-a-half back on. It's a problem keeping it off – the secret is to eat as much as you like, but don't swallow! And I've had to give up some pleasures – I love spaghetti and all that sort of stuff but I had to pack those in. And booze – I don't drink any more.

CLIVE JAMES For twenty years I've been battling with my weight, and I've found out that diets don't work. What you've got to do is change what you eat – and then you can eat as much as you like. I got into fibre, and now I eat carpets and hardboard and the weight just falls off. But I was kind of sick of being overweight and of nothing fitting. Also, I'm fanatical about skiing and being overweight is very bad for that. I mean, you can ski okay, but if you fall down, you can't get up again. I'd fall down, I couldn't get up, snow would accumulate on me and they would find me next spring.

TWIGGY When I was very young and modelling I was very skinny but I had no choice in that, it was just the way I was made. I really was very tiny. After I had my daughter I put on a bit of weight, and now because of my age, and having a family, I think you have to start looking after yourself. So I do tap-dancing classes and I also do very light kind of weights. It just tones you up. There are women who muscle-build but I wouldn't want to do that.

JOANNA LUMLEY I started off modelling in 1964, when mini skirts were the thing, and we had chalk-white faces and three or four layers of eyelashes. We had to be so thin – I'm jealous of the models nowadays who just have to look healthy, tennis-playing girls. In those days, the thickest part of your leg was the knee bone, so all your time was spent trying to be thin and trying not to be spotty. I was a bit spotty – I also had rotten finger nails. In those days they were always breaking so we glued them on. I used to glue them on on the tube going to work. That was OK – people watched with interest. But coming back, when you took them off, men would nearly be sick because it looked so real.

KENNETH WILLIAMS When I was in the Army, they sent me to a Physical Development Centre. The sergeant said, 'You scrawny runts, you've got something to work out at our centre here, and we'll develop you, we'll make sure you leave with bulging muscles.'

One of these is not a dummy. Answers on a postcard please!

Horror, comedy and music in one line-up: Vincent Price, Dudley Moore and Lulu.

David Jason tells Emily Lloyd how much he's looking forward to a glass of LWT wine.

Sean Connery.

And we were shoved on these courses where you had to do all these physical things . . . you had to get on a rope and go across a river and then jump up a fence and go over the other side, it was all that sort of thing. And I just sank in a heap with this rifle on my back and I thought, 'I'm not going to do it, it's awful.' And this sergeant came by on a bicycle – they didn't do any work – and he said, 'What are you doing the dying swan for?' I said, 'No, I can't go on – I'm finished,' and he said 'Rubbish, if you don't do this course, you're here for another 16 weeks and then another one after that until you eventually make it.' I said, 'I couldn't face it, I just can't do it!' And he said, 'All right, get on my cross bar', and we cycled like that and went round back ways and eventually got to a point where he said, 'Jump over that hedge and and say you've done it.' So I did and there was an officer with a clip board and a watch, timing everybody, who said 'Splendid, well done, very well done, Private . . .'

KEEPING TRIM...

GEORGE MELLY There's nothing I detest more than exercise and furthermore, I think it's frightfully bad for you. You're always reading in the obituary columns about joggers. In fact, Jonathan Miller once said that whenever he saw a jogger, he felt that he wasn't jogging for health, he was actually jogging to catch up with his first heart attack.

DOLLY PARTON Jog? Me, jog with these? I'd be afraid I'd black my eyes! But I don't mind what people say about me as long as they know that I've got a brain beneath the wig and a heart beneath the boobs. I make my own jokes about myself – I always say that I'm the only person who left the Smokey Mountains and took them with her.

DENNIS TAYLOR Believe it or not you need to be reasonably fit to play snooker, simply because of the pressures. I mean, a final can last for nine hours and you're on your feet for a long time, and concentrating very hard. So I use an exercise bike and try to keep myself in good shape.

RUBY WAX In this country you don't care if you look old – most of your famous people are dead, what do you care? But in LA you have to have this continuous youthful expression – it's quite frightening. I was frightened that if my behind wasn't hard enough to rebound a tennis ball, they'd shoot me on sight. I went to those aerobics classes sobbing 'Go away cellulite, go away...'

MAUREEN LIPMAN I feel that the best thing to do is to have a really good stretch of a morning. You have to stretch your right hand out completely, and wrap it round a mug of tea, then you have to bring it back to your mouth and drink it. Then I find the best thing to do is to crawl out of bed, across the floor to the bathroom mirror and look at yourself. Crying exercises all the muscles around your face. And then the only other thing you have to do is to walk to the car, get in, and scream at passing natives as you go by.

TALL TALES

The good thing about a joke is that you don't even need an excuse to tell it. Here's a selection of jolly stories from my guests. Some of them are true, some of them aren't – some aren't even jokes at all, I just couldn't bear to leave them out.

Stop me if you've heard this one ...

JIM DAVIDSON A mate of mine was telling me about a fellow, a cockney, who bought a farm down in Cornwall. He was working away in London and he thought he'd ring the foreman down in Cornwall to see how it was all going. 'How's things?' he asked.

'Well, I've got a bit of good news and a bit of bad,' said the foreman.

'What's the bad news?' asked this bloke.

'Your dog's dead,' said the foreman.

'My dog is dead?' said the man. 'How did he die?'

'Well, we're not too sure,' said the foreman. 'We think the horse kicked him.'

'The horse kicked him?' said the man. 'What made the horse frightened, he's normally so placid.'

'Oh, we're not too sure,' said the foreman. 'We think the fire in the barn frightened the horse, and that made him kick the dog.'

'The fire in the barn?' said the man. 'How did the barn catch fire?'

'We're not too sure,' said the foreman. 'We think it may have been a spark from the house.'

'My house has gone?' asked the man. 'How did the house catch fire?'

'Well, we're not certain, but we think it was one of the candles,' said the foreman.

'What candles?' said the man.

'Oh, the ones on your wife's coffin,' said the foreman.

'Well, how did she die?'

'We think it was a heart attack brought on by the fact that your insurance company went bankrupt last week,' said the foreman.

'Isn't there any good news?' asked the man.

'Oh yes,' said the foreman. 'All this heat has brought your tomato plants on a treat.'

GARY WILMOT I'll be quite honest with you – I don't really like jokes. I think they're too contrived – like this one for instance! The telephone rings, a Jewish woman picks up the phone and she says, 'Hello?' And the voice on the other end says, 'I bet you'd like me to kiss you all over your body, I bet you'd like me to massage every muscle on your body, I bet you'd like me to take you upstairs and make mad, passionate love to you.' She said, 'All this you can tell from hello?'

FRANK CARSON Two fellows were playing snooker, and for an hour and a half they hadn't potted a single ball – at which point Paddy says to Mick, 'We'll have to cheat, let's take out the triangle.'

Do you know, there's a club in Johannesburg where they play dominoes and the spots on the dominoes are real diamonds. There was an Irishman playing there recently and he took a double-blank.

Maggie Murphy was singing in the front row of the choir when she overbalanced and fell. She was hurtling down into the middle of the church when the leg of her knickers caught on one of the rafters. There she was, swinging up and down, and the kind priest said, 'If any man turns round and looks at that unfortunate woman, may the Lord strike him blind.' And Paddy turns to Flannigan and says, 'I think I'll risk the one eye . . .'

DAVE ALLEN I heard a story about the Sisters of Mercy in New York, who are finding it hard to survive because they exist totally on donations. They have a place in the dock and the red light area and they help the drunks and the ladies of the night. And one nun, as a joke, said, 'Wouldn't it be fun to put a red light outside the Convent to see what it would attract.' So they thought, yes, and they put a discreet red light outside and they stationed one of the nuns in the corridor and about two hours later, the door opened and a man said, 'How much?'

'Two hundred dollars,' said the nun.

'Two hundred dollars?' said the man. 'What am I going to get for that?'

'Well, you can have a Sister of Mercy – it's quite different,' she said.

So he put down the money and she said, 'Go past the chapel, up the stairs, turn left at the corridor and go through a door.' So he did all that, but when he opened the door, he found himself back on the street and the door behind him was self-locking. He turned round and was kicking hell out of this door, and then he saw, written on the door, a notice which said, 'You have just been screwed by the Sisters of Mercy.'

MEL BROOKS Two cowboys see an Indian lying flat in the road with his ear pressed to the ground. 'He's listening,' said the cowboy. 'He can hear something in the road.' One of the cowboys bends over and says, 'What are you doing?' The Indian says, 'Coach – stage coach – six horses, four white and two black...' 'That's amazing,' said the cowboy. And the Indian went on 'Two men ride on top, one look like Gabby Hayes with shot gun, the other man handsome – could be leading man...' And the cowboys were terribly impressed. 'He sticks his ear to the ground, he can hear four white horses, two black horses, Gabby Hayes with a shotgun, a good-looking other guy – how does he do it?' And the Indian says, 'No, no, you got it all wrong. They came by twenty minutes ago, ran me over, left me like this.' That's one of my favourites.

BOB NEWHART An Englishman arrives in the States at JFK Airport, and he gets in a taxi. The cab driver's from Brooklyn and he said to the Englishman, 'Do you enjoy riddles?' 'Yes, I do actually,' said the Englishman. 'In fact it's my favourite form of humour.' So the driver said, 'OK, my mother had a child, and it wasn't my brother and it wasn't my sister – who was it?' And the Englishman said, 'Let me think now – it wasn't your brother and it wasn't your sister – I can't imagine.' And the taxi driver says, 'It was me!' So the

Englishman gets back to London and he said to a friend, 'I heard an amusing riddle when I was in the States. My mother had a child, and it wasn't my brother and it wasn't my sister – who was it?' And his friend said, 'I can't imagine.' And the Englishman said, 'It was a cab driver in Brooklyn.'

NICHOLAS LYNDHURST This chap is driving home – sober – and he's pulled over by a police car. The policeman steps out of a patrol car, taps on the window – 'Would you like to step out of the car, sir?' So the driver got out, and he said, 'I haven't been drinking, Officer, really, I'm just on my way home.' So the policeman said, 'Don't worry about that, sir, if you'd just like to follow me round the back of the car, please.' So he goes round the back of the car and he says, 'Defective brake light,' and this chap looks at the brake light and just falls down on his knees and says, 'Oh God, what am I going to do, I don't believe it, how can it have happened?' And the policeman says, 'Well, I shouldn't worry over-much, sir, it's just a brake light.' And the driver said, 'Never mind about the brake light – where's my caravan?'

JULIE CHRISTIE I actually got expelled from school for telling this joke – it's so pathetic, it really is. A man and a woman were travelling in a train and the woman gets up and says, 'Excuse me, I have to go and powder my nose.' So she left the carriage and came back after a short while, and then the man gets up, and he says, 'Excuse me, but I have to go and powder my nose.' And he left and when he came back, she said, 'Oh sir, you've left your compact open and the lipstick's showing . . .!'

DENIS NORDEN It would be rather nice if you could tag jokes, like they tag birds, and then follow their migratory path. You know, tell a joke here, and then tag it and see how soon it turns up in Scarborough or wherever.

PRACTICAL JOKES...

TERRY JONES I can remember my first joke, which must have been when I was two or three. We were all sitting around the tea table in

Colwyn Bay and my grandmother said would I like some more custard. So I thought, as a joke, that I'd pass my mat up. And of course my grandmother takes the mat and pours custard over it. I was thrilled, I thought it was brilliant, but nobody else was laughing. They all said, 'What did you do that for, you stupid boy?' and gave me a clip around the earhole, so I gave up jokes.

ARTHUR MARSHALL They were fairly stuffy in the Army. I remember there was one poor Major who really had no sense of humour at all, and looked gloomy the whole day through. I kept trying to cheer him up but nothing happened. So one day, he came up to me and he said, 'I say, everybody in this headquarters seems to be using Christian names – what's yours?' Well, I've got three initials and the first one is 'C', so I said, 'My name's Cynthia.' 'That's a bloody silly name for a man,' said the Major, and I said, 'Yes, isn't it?' But anyway he continued to call me Cynthia for quite some time – 'I say Cynthia, the General wants you,' and things like that. And eventually, I said, 'You really will have to give up calling me Cynthia – people are talking!'

VINCENT PRICE The first 3D picture I made was called *The House of Wax*, and in it, I dipped everybody in wax and then hung them up in my museum. I used to love going to sit at the back of the cinema where it was showing – preferably behind a couple of teenage girls because their reactions were marvellous. They'd watch this thing, absolutely glued to it in horror, and then one day, at the very end of the film after I'd just fallen into a vat of boiling wax, I leaned forward to the girls, and very quietly said, 'Did you like it?' The popcorn shot up in the air – in fact they tell me that the girls were never seen again . . .

JIMMY TARBUCK In my show I sometimes do a Tom Jones impersonation, and when I was doing it in Nottingham once, I was really going for it, swinging the microphone, when it came right off the lead, shot in the air and a fellow in the audience caught it, thank God, before it did any damage. So afterwards I was a bit worried about it, and I said to the band, 'Look, I won't do Tom Jones tomorrow night, OK?' So the next night we're all set and someone says, 'Phone call for you, Jimmy.' So I went to the stage door, and I waited and waited but there was nobody there. So I was a bit annoyed and I said to the door man, 'Don't call me if there's no one on the phone.' Then I went into the dressing-room, got changed and went on stage. And I'm in the middle of the act when all of a sudden the band starts doing the Tom Jones number, and I had to go through with it. And then I looked at the audience and saw all the people in the first few rows were wearing those helmets they wear on building sites! A comedian called Bernie Clifton had collected them and given them to the audience while I was waiting by the phone.

NIGEL HAVERS I did something to my dad once which was awful, and I regretted it bitterly afterwards, but you know how it is when you think of a good wind-up. When I was home one weekend, I went up the phone box, rang home and pretended I was from *Panorama*, and that we were coming to do an interview. When I got home Dad said, 'You won't believe this but the BBC are coming to do another interview.' 'Oh really?' I said, and left it at that. It was a very hot summer's day, and Dad got into a suit and tie, and he remained like that all day. So I went back to the phone booth and said, 'I'm terribly sorry, we seem to be a bit lost.' So he gave me instructions to get to my own house – it was terribly funny. And at 5 o'clock, he said, 'Those bloody people still aren't here,' and I said, 'It was me...' There was just silence, and then he said, 'Get me a large whisky,' and he never mentioned it again.

JUDI DENCH In *Mother Courage* there's a scene where I had to give a drink to two soldiers, played by Paul Clayton and Paul Greenwood and they had to give me the money for it – which I then bit and put in my pocket. Well, at the last matinee, I gave them the drink, but when they should have handed me the money, they gave me an American Express card instead – I managed not to laugh, in fact I hardly batted an eyelid. But what they didn't know was that after that show, I treated the drink. So in the evening, when they actually did have the proper money, the drink that they had to throw back was cider vinegar. And the glorious thing was that they had to ask me for another!'

BELIEVE IT OR NOT...

PAT PHOENIX We got all sorts of letters sent to us at *Coronation Street*. One came from a vicar and it said, 'Dear Madam, my organ has recently collapsed and I would like your assistance in raising it . . .'

LENNY HENRY I went to Dublin recently. The taxi drivers are just hilarious. I got in and the driver said, 'Are you that Lenny Henry?' 'Yes,' I said. 'Get away, you bugger,' he said. 'You don't look anything like him!' He made me laugh so much that I gave him twenty pounds – the fare was only four.

GEORGE COLE After we had been doing *Minder* for about two years we were sitting in a car, Dennis Waterman was in the front with someone and I was sitting in the back. Dennis was talking about a film he had been in called *Fright*. And I said, 'You weren't in that.' He said, 'I was.' I said, 'You weren't – *I* was in that!' He said, 'You weren't.' Well, it turned out we were both in it but I hadn't realized who he was because he played the part of a man who was murdered very early on, and spent the entire film lying on his face on the floor – and I kept stepping over him.

DAVID JASON A couple of years ago I was having a party with some friends, and one of them went out of the house to the car to get something, and she felt this great lick on her hand and it was a stray dog, starved and very, very frightened. Anyway, I put little scraps out for it over the next week, and it wouldn't go away. It had got a damaged foot with a sort of bandage round it so we went down to the vet some weeks later because it wasn't getting any better, and they said, 'Sorry, but you either put the dog down or you have its leg off.' So I thought, 'Well, it's best to cut its leg off and see if it survives – give it a chance, why not?' The vet was pretty convinced that it would be all right. So they bring the dog back after a couple of days and the poor little thing's looking terrible, its eyes are out on organ stops. It comes in about 4 o'clock in the afternoon and at 4 o'clock the next morning we're both standing like this, saying, 'Please go to bed, doggy, go back to bed.' This dog stood for twenty-four hours on three legs. I was up all night – it wouldn't go to bed because of the pain. So I phoned up the vet the next day, I felt so sorry for the dog. The vet comes round and he says, 'Look, I'll give her a big jab so she can get some sleep and she'll be out in ten minutes.' He gets the bottle into the dog, twenty minutes later the dog's still going, so he says, 'I can't understand it, I can't believe this,' he says, 'I've given her a huge dose but this one will knock her out.' An hour later we're still looking at this dog. And the vet said, 'I can't understand this,' he said, 'I just can't understand it. I've given her enough to knock a horse out,' he said, 'it just won't close its eyes.' I said, 'Can you blame it – the last time it closed its eyes it woke up with one leg missing.'

KENNY EVERETT I loved a story I heard on the radio about the days when Britain owned India and one of the colonels who'd been there was talking about his chef, who used to live at the bottom of the garden. He said, 'Our chef made the most amazingly round dumplings – they were perfect, and I always wondered how he did it but he wouldn't tell me – it was a secret. So one day I crept down the lawn and looked in the shed, and I saw him rolling these dumplings – in his armpits! And do you know I've never been able to face one since.'

DAVID FROST It's difficult to top some people, like the guy who had been struck by lightning six times and by the time we found him he'd been struck a seventh time. He worked – rather foolishly, I thought – as a park ranger – not the perfect career, I felt. And down in Brazil we met the woman with the greatest number of children – thirty-three – and no multiple births – no cheating! We interviewed her, then we interviewed her husband. And when he got up, he said, 'Yes, I am married to this woman, with her I've had thirty-three children. But I've had three outside romances through which I've had a further ninety-two children!'

JULIE CHRISTIE When we filmed *Dr Zhivago*, it was supposed to be St Petersburg in midwinter – in fact, it was Madrid in a freak heatwave. There we were, waiting for this multi-million dollar epic to be made while sweating away in our furs in 100 degrees heat. Finally we were saved by the props and set dressers who covered the whole of the set in mountains of marble dust – for the long shots, the fields were covered in miles and miles of bed sheets. I think the villagers were a little perplexed by this, but we fooled you, didn't we?

HARRY ENFIELD ('Stavros') Hello, everybody peeps. Is-a very nice to be here on *Asp and Com* for a little bit of shit-shat with Michael. You know, I remember Michael when he used to do the BBC *Ten to Nine News* way, way, way back long time since. You remember this? 'This is Michael Aspel with the news. Today Mr Hitler is invade Poland.' Then of course after that he went a little big crazy-bonk for a while cause he change his name to Ask, *Ask Aspel*. I don't understand. And then at last he finally reached the biggest challenge of his life trying to get a word of sense out of Oliver Reed, you know, the well-known teetote I'm-a don't think. And now of course he just been offered for to take over the job of Eamonn Andrews presenting *That's Life* and I'm glad about this because it's my favourite prog, in it. Apart from of course my other favourite prog is Leslie Crackerjack Pense Crowth with *Come On Down Mrs Smith How Much It Bloody Well Cost?* But my wife, her inside indoors, right, she like the more intelligent show games like his Holiness Bob Blockbuster – you know this? '"C" please, Bob, "B" please, Bob.' But I'm-a always like it best when they say 'I'm-a think I like to have a "P" please, Bob', it always make me chuck, it is. The TV quiz I'm-a best at myself though is *A Quest of Sport*, but the trouble with this one is I'm-a don't like Emily Hughes – you know him, Emily Hughes, he's a bit thick, in it. You know, David Coleman is say something like 'Well, I can't do very well but I have a go,' in it. 'Er – Emily – er – who is won the football worly cup in 1966. Oh I knows it, I knows it, oh come on team.' He's-a bloody squeaky voice git, in it. What I'm-a should have is Keith Harris should get rid of little Orville and get Emily Hughes instead. 'Hello Emily – Hello Keith.' Goodnight, peeps.

Aspel: I've read that you once drank 104 pints in 24 hours – is it true?

Oliver Reed: No, it was 48 hours.

Aspel: Oh well, that's all right then.